The Art of identity

The Art of identity

**creating and managing
a successful corporate identity**

mark rowden

Gower

Published by
Gower Publishing Limited
Gower House
Croft Road
Aldershot
Hampshire GU11 3HR
England

Gower
131 Main Street
Burlington
Vermont 05401
USA

British Library Cataloguing in Publication Data
Rowden, Mark
    The art of identity : creating and managing a
    successful identity
    1. Corporate image 2. Corporate image –
        Psychological aspects
    I. Title
    659.2'85

ISBN 0 566 08318 3

Designed by Mark Rowden.
Printed in Great Britain by
The University Press, Cambridge.

Contents

Preface

Issues surrounding the role of identity have reached the stage where more explanation is not only beneficial but essential if the debate about the subject is to be advanced. A firmer and more precise framework is needed for all those who wish to benefit from using design—which ought to include everybody, certainly in management—and for the education of all those who operate within its boundaries.

The overall strategy of an organisation is directly connected to its identity, and every marketing or communication element must be purposefully and effectively sprung from that central point. Many identity projects start life as almost impenetrably confusing: a new ambitious organisation or product launch; the new technology no one is entirely sure how to market; an identity that has seriously gone awry; the organisation taking over or being taken over; the young or established organisation struggling to define itself; and many other scenarios besides. Each project presents itself differently, yet the threads that run between each identity problem and its successful solution remain similar. The fundamental issues remain the same, though they may seem invisible to most. Perhaps they are simply inexplicable to all but the most visually literate: those designers who often quietly solve the problems regardless of client or studio management; and perhaps they in turn cannot readily articulate their insight.

As a design consultant who has chosen always to work independently, I have been able to progress my approach, and my system of beliefs, in response to the realities of one-to-one consulting with a highly diverse range of organisations. Many of these are based in the economic boom area of Cambridge, an area rich in unusually creative, mostly high technology businesses, led by many unusual minds, and a few geniuses, making it all the more fascinating.

Idealistic though it is, my priority has been forging the type of often very personal client relationships that I believe are the best: creative partnerships which allow no unnecessary obstacles between the creativity required and the problem to be solved. Continually drawn into an exceptionally wide range of design and identity projects, I aim to select projects according to the integrity and purpose of the client, whatever the challenges or difficulties presented by their desires, objectives, brief or any other form of restriction.

To write about identity in any worthwhile way is difficult. This book is a response to the frustrating gulf which so often opens up between the designer and the client organisation. Writing it is partly the result of needing to analyse and describe what I have so often left unexplained or unjustified—usually because a client or fellow worker has let me escape without proper explanation. I hope it helps readers to create, manage and sustain an identity, as well as offering the means to probe and evaluate the identity of another.

As so often happens, the idea of a book began with something someone said, in this case by Sue Wallis during a conversation one spring morning at LaserScan, Cambridge. It seemed such a casual and minor aside that she probably does not recall it. Discussions continued through a progression of what others also said and, on occasions, didn't! Willing and unwitting contributors, to name but a few, have included the crucial and encouraging Philip Taylor (product designer and consultant), Richard Longdon and Steven Talbott (Cadcentre), Martin Sebborn (Spectreview), John Barker (Grant Instruments), the most helpful, spirited and spiritual advisor Geoff Dodgson (Chamberlain Partnership), the philosophical eagle eye of Bob Seymore (photographer), and the astute editing of Suzie Duke.

Acknowledgement is also due to the Watford College of Printing and Packaging, now known as West Herts College Faculty of Visual Communication, where, as an artist, I enlisted to study typographic design under the supervision of Os Turner, Mike Matthews and the influential Howard Patterson.

That was in the days when a sharp pencil and a crisp brain were the only computers available. Now, with high-tech tools and communication channels, an organisation's identity and the principles that underpin it are predictably becoming more decisive and crucial than ever. We live in an age in which we are pounded with information, and amongst this din and clutter an identity needs to speak with clarity and purpose.

The Art of Identity is written for individuals and organisations, whoever or whatever you are, professional, student, creative or less so. To know more about identity is to know more about yourself. This means having a willingness to sit back and think: a rare commodity in such a hurrying age. I hope that this book offers you the opportunity to do just that.

Instinct

What is identity?

Ultimately, all identity is a lie. This is because identity is a mask you choose to wear; or it is a mask you choose to see. As such, it appears as a fixed image within an otherwise moving world.

That is not to say that an identity should not attempt to be truthful. It is an acknowledgement that people and organisations are in a permanent state of change, and the image they wish to project may be at variance with the truth of where they are today. Indeed, their image may be the intention of what they want to be or how they wish to be seen. Truly effective identity manages this 'reality gap', promoting a set of deliberate messages and providing sufficient flexibility for the identity to grow with the individual or organisation's growth.

Thought—there are identifiable laws regarding identity.

These laws have, within the limits of your audience, controllable aspects. You have a choice to deliberately determine the 'reality gap' of your identity, or leave it to chance.

The most obvious benefit of identity is being seen, and more, being seen to be different. Difference makes you visible and separates your personality from others. But difference is not enough. Your differential must attract, motivate and propel the instincts of those around you in accordance with your ambitions.

Many organisations are content to believe that their logo, and little else, is their identity. However, this is a shallow assumption, for a logo, albeit often the most visible graphic element, indicates only part of an overall identity. Successful identity is planned to succeed at all levels of communication. Only then does an organisation communicate an identity that ensures success and steers away from failure. Be aware that an unsuitable identity can only mislead and obstruct the wearer, and that a complete lack of any planned identity produces worse: the unknown and, inevitably, the undesirable.

A complete identity should cover all aspects of visual, written and spoken communication—no road or avenue you are about to proceed down should remain unaddressed. This is as challenging for you as it will be for your audience. If an identity represents opportunity, it also signals limitations: if we are to know who we are, we must equally know who we are not. Understanding your purpose and beliefs, then managing them with flair and accuracy, can be a private matter for an individual—a lone dancer controls his or her own movements. But the larger the organisation, the more difficult it is to maintain the choreography: stricter direction is required and, hence, it is important to enshrine all aspects of the identity into a written manual. This creates the focus, measuring stick and point of discussion—as all identity must have a review process in order to avoid the traps of time.

Thought—to avoid chance, application and commitment are required.

Achieving a successful identity is not for either the faint-hearted or fuzzy-minded. And clarity together with depth of vision is essential before you apply creativity.

Belief

If you believe in yourself you should believe in your identity. In addition, an appearance favourable to your aims and beliefs needs to represent more than merely a surface. The same principles should permeate deeper, so that the identity that is seen always keeps its promise. We can all think of manufacturers who have used the past beliefs and reputation of a badge or marque on an inferior new product. When the truth is realised, the customer (and staff) feel cheated. Once cheated, the memory of dissatisfaction persists for a considerable time, if not forever.

Identifying your core beliefs is no easy matter—but identify you must, for if you don't know, how can you expect your market area to know? Insist on knowing who you are and where you are going. Failure to identify these beliefs produces an unpredictability which, in turn, will inevitably produce a shortfall in understanding and communication. This failure can easily spread throughout service, product design, manufacture and personnel, finally impacting upon the entire venture and its level of profit or loss.

To become successful, a team must share the same core beliefs. That team will feel energised in the knowledge that their contribution to the whole, whether major or minor, knowingly fits within the aims and beliefs of the overall venture. They will also project these shared beliefs as one. In this respect, a smaller organisation has an advantage over a larger one when it comes to punching beyond its weight. A vision is more easily shared and can therefore become so much more powerful within a smaller team.

Your beliefs need to communicate themselves to your audience without confusing them. All good interpretation requires an allowance for others' emotions. You need to communicate often with those who have no intention of communicating with you. Will you mislead, repel or attract them? If you attract them, will it be for the correct reasons? Likewise, if you repel them.

Thought—belief and ambition should be detailed, known and communicated throughout an organisation.

An identity should adhere to these beliefs and ambitions if it is to contribute towards its aims, rather than hinder them.

Emotion

How can we learn to understand the instincts and emotions of our audience?

We need to reflect upon our own instincts in order to understand others. We may prefer our personal self-image as that of someone unmoved by emotional reactions to such things as the appearance of people, products, advertisements or environments—for example buildings and their interiors. We may pride ourselves that we have the ability or experience to 'see through' and decide for ourselves the salient information and truth that we seek. However, the reality is that we are all, some more than others, susceptible to our emotions and passions. And it is in this morass of emotion versus reason that an identity must operate and succeed. That is why appearances are so critically important.

People tend to believe what they see. We all share a great tendency to judge the contents by the container. Moreover, we do this with a careless urgency. For example, when your audience meets you for the first time, or encounters your publicity material, they will attempt to evaluate you as speedily as they can, so they may proceed—with or without you. You had better assume that any audience is impatient and has a limited attention span. Their desire will be to label you, and identify and file this image with some urgency. Likewise, you will be evaluating them. These snap judgements will follow a mixture of conscious and unconscious reason and emotion. And they will be quick: a few seconds or a few minutes. While the clock is running, each increment of time will make your first impressions recede into history. In other words, unless you start from the correct position of identity, your failure will proceed, and compound, at the rate of one second per second. History will become track record, and track record, eventually, will become the reality of your relationship.

Any audience will judge what you say against how you appear. Upon this simple judgement they will be inclined to base their trust or distrust. Ask yourself whether they will believe what you say about yourself when they compare it with what they can see. Realise that their reaction to what they see is likely to be the main influence over their first impressions.

What people see is both rapidly and largely automatically processed by their minds. They may not be exercising any concentrated or conscious reason whilst they gaze in your direction, but they are assessing you at the speed of light. They, you, cannot help this process.

Instincts are powerful forces, for they have a tendency to sweep away everything from their path. To succeed in building a relationship with your audience, their instincts must be either confirmed or overthrown.

This level of negotiation is greater than you may initially think; destiny is often decided from the first moment of contact.

To demonstrate the power of instincts, spend a few moments completing Tests 1 and 2. Test 1 is overleaf.

Test 1

Imagine that the three shapes illustrated opposite are logos, each representing a major banking organisation.

■ In your opinion, which bank
   is the most forward-looking?

■ In your opinion, which bank
   will take the greatest risk with your investments?

■ In your opinion, which bank
   has been established the greatest number of years?

Bank A

Bank B

Bank C

Test 2

For this test, examine the colour illustration on the inside front cover.

The coloured shapes are the logos and colours
of competing motor-racing teams.

- In your opinion, which motor-racing team
  enjoys the fastest lap times?

- In your opinion, which motor-racing team
  is the most technically advanced?

- In your opinion, which driver
  has the most reliable car?

You may be surprised at your reactions to these simple tests. Your
initial responses will probably defy a wholly rational explanation.
However, they will confirm or deny your preferences and prejudices
regarding both shape and colour. You should therefore realise that
the only correct answer to the questions in both tests is our tendency
to make emotional judgements beyond any conscious reason. Yet
there is a level of computation at work here, for your opinion has
been influenced by the use of shape and colour.

An identity exists within a confusing and emotional market area. It
is therefore vital to create and manage an identity's purpose,
strength and effectiveness. The leap from instinctive and emotional
first impressions to logical or consciously reasoned opinion is an
unpredictable process. An excellent identity succeeds in managing
this process effectively. A poor identity does not.

Courage

Recognition and confrontation

Imagine you are an infant in a crowded classroom. You impulsively thrust your hand up into the air. If the teacher acknowledges this signal for attention, and invites your contribution, you must then continue past the initial plea for attention and communicate with confidence and clarity if you want to make the most of the opportunity. As well as ability, this takes nerve, both of which you may be fortunate enough to take for granted.

Courage plays a major part in the willingness to be identified and one's effectiveness beyond the initial threshold of recognition. It means inviting reaction from all those who notice your signal. Personally, you may be able to brush these concerns away more readily than other members of your team, but the point remains that it takes courage to state your opinions and hold onto your values.

Thought—identity needs to be able to defend itself.

Your fear of being challenged and the controversy you are prepared to engage in is largely within your control. You can avoid both by adopting a low profile. There may be good reason for modesty, but, whatever your preference, you appear to be able to choose accordingly—or can you?—for even the silent get labelled. And the silent really are the majority. Not all are prepared to believe in their values, opinions and ability to argue and defend themselves, even when it may be to their great advantage. Fear rules most people all too readily. Far easier for the timid or unconfident to dissolve their identity into the mass of the crowd, to follow a trend, any trend, and thoughtlessly imitate other individuals or organisations whose clothes they'd rather be seen to wear.

How willing you are to draw attention to yourself, by which method and in what preferred manner you wish to deal with the inevitable responses are a direct reflection upon your ability and confidence.

Perhaps you may prefer less intrusive methods of communication? Or perhaps being within a crowd lends you strength and comfort? Perhaps being a me-too offers you the level of profit you wish or are willing to settle for? Or perhaps you find the reverse is true? What is certain is that you engage in the level and type of confrontation you feel confident enough to be challenged by.

Being identified leads to confrontation simply because your identity will inevitably confront the identity, feelings and opinions of others. Your willingness to assert a bold and highly visible identity may be tempered by your fear of being challenged. And these challenges are not just external ones. Inside the organisation, the short-sighted, the ill-informed and fearful alike may challenge an existing, revised or brand new identity which they believe threatens their dependency, position or personal advantage.

Thought—difference threatens the insecure.

How well you manage these challenges is determined by your trust in yourself. Self-trust could be explained as trusting the ground you stand upon. You may say you want an effective identity: if so, get ready for the occasional attack, for you will rarely stand unchallenged.

Seeking a new identity challenges you before anybody else. This form of self-destruction, for in part any form of renewing involves challenging or destroying the old, can be as depressing as it is liberating. You engage with the probability of change, and in this new-found and freefall freedom lurks infinite possibility. There are many right and wrong turnings—as well as a definite sense of vacuum: everything that you discover and choose to abandon creates new space longing to be filled. It takes a suspension of belief to accept this space, however temporary (it usually is), for 'nothing' is acutely uncomfortable to those driven by habit first, thought second. It means stopping or stepping off—which promotes insecurity—the flip side of which is freedom. If you are serious about your mission, it is a heroic struggle against the pressures of current routine, attitudes and dogma. It is not surprising that creating and launching a new identity is, for many, a traumatic experience, a crisis compounded by the difficulty of establishing a new excellence amongst the ruins of the old. Get tough on yourself and your weaknesses, or fail. Gamble on your ability to make the right decisions. Apply rigour and set off to search for and study the justification for all that pretends to belong to your current identity.

Thought—you cannot escape identification.

With an unplanned identity, you may have only a scant idea of the reactions you provoke. Inconsistency in the signals you transmit may draw an equally inconsistent array of responses. Alternatively, with a planned identity, you should expect more certain reactions: because if you regulate the messages on offer to others, you should find, over time, the responses received in return will fall into patterns and, more crucially, patterns that you will have the opportunity to become well acquainted with. This information you accrue becomes a further confirmation of your certainty. This certainty clarifies the risks you can typically expect and, with these informed expectations, the defences you need to deploy—in economy of time, energy and material. The introduction of a planned identity rapidly enables easier progress. But, like learning a new musical instrument, it requires a period of commitment and discomfort, which as a novice, introducing yourself to your new self, you now have no choice but to pass through. However uncomfortable this is, you must commit yourself to the process of relearning.

Thought—it is fear of being recognised as different, whatever the rhetoric to the contrary, that prevents many from achieving the identity to match what they state is their ambition.

Often the identities, and in particular the logos, within many sectors of activity appear to converge. The more competitive the subject area, the greater the tendency towards convergence: for example political parties and national flags, but also most retail product areas, such as food packaging and automotive design. They gravitate towards conformity through fear of appearing too different. Conformity is a comforting magnet. If questioned, and in their defence, these organisations may feel that they are promoting themselves in this manner in order to avoid alienating their target audiences. In other words, they are acknowledging convention, or the notion of convention, as their guiding master. But often an audience may not be as aware, or as concerned, about these conventions as the communicator of the identity believes. Indeed, it may be the identity seeking comfort under the false pretence of comforting the audience. There is always the chance that the audience is yearning to abandon the humdrum conformity before them, but only the very brave will give them the opportunity.

Those who defy the conventional boundaries take the risk of temporary or lasting ridicule, or abject failure. Those who succeed are recognised as redefining the market boundaries, often to massive acclaim—though always post-rationalised, for they took a risk that others either could not see, or could not take at the time. And so others follow.

When attempting to challenge boundaries, sincerity in effort and belief—product development, design and service—is a useful, if not a necessary, ingredient. A nonentity or 'non-identity', is an identity of fake, mismatched or dubious values, which rarely remains undetected for long. You only have to look around most town centres to realise that the number of nonentities massively outnumbers the presence of the genuine article. Regrettably most identities fail through just such insincerity of effort and belief.

Illustration 1

same	same	same
same	same	same
same	same	different
same	same	same
same	same	same
same	same	same
same	same	same

We are all drawn to difference. It finds our attention.

Thought—to be eligible for something better, you need to consider the risks.

Risk

Those eligible for effective identity become conversant with measuring the nature of the risks they are prepared to engage themselves and their organisation in.

To reach the highest levels of competitive performance, you must not only approach these risks willingly, but explore them thoroughly. The boundaries these risks appear to threaten may be negotiable: the perception of risk alters the apparent opportunities which lie before you. It is both necessary and worthwhile to examine your current perceptions and test them in order to validate their reality. Creating a new identity involves confronting and challenging your notion of the existing, and repositioning what was previously considered immovable.

Decisions must create risks, however seemingly inconsequential, and deciding to examine an existing identity or forge a new one is rife with them. The first decision is to elect to take the chance in the first place. Assuming you do, and that all proceeds well, can you understand and manage the resultant success? If the opportunity arises, have you the courage to achieve something notable and, having achieved it, the eyes to see it and the ability to manage it?

The truth is that many individuals and organisations do not deserve a successful identity, simply because of the inability of their management. Sadly, some would not recognise good identity under almost any circumstances. Designers often lament to one another that their best designs are under threat of being rejected. If they are refused, that must be partly their fault for lack of persuasion—or else they merely whinge. Certainly, some do, but the truth must be that those who employ them do so because they do not possess the same level of visual awareness themselves, however astute they may otherwise be. It is commonplace for those in business to recognise

Illustration 2

different

different

different

different

different

different

different

different

different

Everybody can claim to be different. Those that actually are stand out clearly.

the successful identities of others—normally the obviously successful—but have no understanding of how to achieve the same. Many
fail to trust themselves or those they employ—a double blow if you
also pay their wages. Usually they fail to exercise the necessary
courage to lead the team they choose to surround themselves with
assertively enough.

Thought—good leaders liberate those who surround them.

In the same way, good clients release the talents of the designers
they employ. If fortunate, they both may have the mettle to explore
and share the results of their experimentation together and, in
doing so, form a partnership of equality and unusual opportunity.

Thought—you surround yourself with the team you deserve.

You may think you deserve more, or less, but how can you be sure?
Who you surround yourself with broadcasts your personal level of
confidence and ability. Assuming the choice is yours to make, what
criteria have you chosen in the process of this selection: family and
friendship, levels of professional skill, age, sex, quality of aggression,
ego (yours or theirs), no criteria at all or considerations of budget?
Perhaps the best people actually scare you; it's worth asking yourself
the question. The idea is to prick your pride, push yourself around a
little, get rough, tip your pockets out, have a good laugh at your own
expense, mock yourself, detach yourself from the current situation
as far as possible, and be determined that you will attempt to see
more clearly. It is time to check the view outside by attempting to
look in, see yourself through the eyes of those whom you choose to
surround yourself with. Confused? Don't worry, it is all part of the
process of self-examination.

Thought—the companion of success is failure.

Failure is worth daily examination. Truly creative people know this
better than most: the possible wrong, the apparent mistake or the
half-workable may represent the halfway house to the ridiculous, or

sublime. Being criticised, rebuked, or worse, can be everyday experiences for those prepared to voice their ideas. They look risk directly in the eyes and work with it in the interests of producing the remarkable, the exceptional. Examining defeat does not mean choosing failure as a route, it means looking for the finer entrances or opportunities that nobody else has been prepared to search for or had the ability to spot

Thought—the solution you seek is likely to be beyond the reflection you see in your mirror.

The elusive solution that offers the substantial progress you or your organisation may be looking for is often beyond what you see immediately before you. If you are blinded by the reflection it is only because you haven't challenged that reflection enough, or tried moving the mirror. You ought to disbelieve more often and attempt to view events from other perspectives. Don't be afraid to make a fool of yourself. Excessive pride is the biggest single barrier to advancement. Fear of failure rides shotgun.

The experienced know they cannot go through life expecting and experiencing only success. At some point we must deal with failure too. Why do we expect all our thoughts to be positive, when negative must surely, by the law of nature, be an average fifty per cent of the equation? It is worth bearing in mind that often the most spectacular and creative solutions arise because an apparently negative situation prompts a positive one.

Acknowledging that this sliding scale between success and failure stands before you, whatever journey you and your intrepid team embark upon, would suggest that navigation of some sort is a sensible idea. With every objective there are choices of departure point and route. Preparation is advisable. A potentially treacherous route is rendered more secure by a map, however sketchy. Suitable clothing and mode of transport should be selected together with enough resources and time for the journey. If you are choosing to employ a driver, a navigator or an entire support crew of mechanics, choose them with care. With equal care, plan your journey. Though it may sound obvious, this standard of planning should match the standard of the objective. It is no good attempting a trip to Saturn on a bicycle when a rocket ship would seem more suitable. But even assuming you can build the propulsion unit or find someone who can sell you one, have you the ability to pilot this exotic but necessary projectile?

If not, decide against an unsuitable journey. Simply do not start. Stand still, rip the map up, retreat to base, pack up or plan another route instead. Perhaps the original destination is too ambitious to manage in one go. A three-year journey cannot fit into a day—so prepare accordingly. You cannot afford to be excessively hopeful or pessimistic. You are seeking your own new realism. Comfort or discomfort, judgement is everything.

Thought—sitting comfortably can be hazardous.

Beware of feeling too comfortable. The comfort of security tends to disable the capacity to react, weakening the will to make the correct changes. Comfort often makes risk appear far less tempting. Indeed, comfort may seriously hamper your ability to see and judge accurately at all. Some organisations appear to change for change's sake, perhaps because budget is not currently an issue, or they feel led by the pressure of fashion. That is fine providing they are not blind to the risks. The benefits of worthwhile change may remain invisible to others; some may believe they do not exist at all. Either way, to find out, the only means of transportation is risk, unless another has already blazed the trail. The hopes and aspirations of the crew and passengers may not match—even though you may officially declare the same destination—but have you the belief to trust your instinct and action what you believe is necessary, regardless of the opposition? If you do not already consider yourself to be an accomplished leader, you now have an urgent need to become one.

Leadership

Issues of leadership—internal

Authority

The authority of leadership and identity are closely dependent upon each other. Leadership is necessary for the initiation of an identity programme, implementation and successful outcome. Identity labours towards defining the authority of the organisation or product and those who lead it.

The full commitment of the leader, or leadership, of an organisation is essential if an identity programme is to succeed. The quality of the identity and the objectives of the organisation must, if they are to have any credence, work together. An identity demands support from the highest authority within the organisation to make this a certainty.

Truth

Truth demands management. This is the divide between the mask you intend to present to your audience, and the actual reality or experience of product or service you offer them.

Thought—promise or reality, one leads the other.

For some organisations and products, the quality of the experience they offer exceeds the promise of their appearance. In other words they are noticeably better than the promise of their identity. In such cases the harm is a self-inflicted lost opportunity, or margin. Those clients that accept yet know the shortcomings of such an organisation's identity may be bemused or enthused by their 'discovery'. They may spread the word or keep the secret—either through lack of self-confidence, or fear that rising demand might destroy the source—because they consider the organisation is unable to sustain the subsequent growth, or the potential of mass popularity offends their taste anyway. Meanwhile, the organisation in question may have less need for celebration. Failure to understand the merits and pitfalls of the existing identity make it perilous to move forwards without endangering its reputation still further.

For other organisations these roles can be reversed: their identity promises too much. This can be forgiven, providing it is also credible—the gap between the promise and the reality is understandable or bearable because the promise remains sincere. Of course, patience can only be stretched so far. When waiting or enduring can be stood no more, and those disappointed finally flee, persuading them to return may be a lengthy and difficult exercise.

Managing the gap

Your integrity, the soundness or corruption of your identity in the eyes and ears of the audience, is determined by how well you manage this duality. The danger arises when the break is, or appears to be, unsustainable. A tired or cynical audience may reach a point where they become convinced that the divide is too large to close—the beginnings of a potentially major identity crisis. To recover, you must understand the problem and be prepared to react quickly for, if the disbelief threatens to be permanent, the identity becomes, at best, instantly ineffectual, negative or fatal.

Hence the importance of remaining knowledgeable about yourself, your organisation, audience and identity, because knowledge is an advantage over circumstance and competition. Learning must be a continual process of adaptation through enquiry and experience. No true leader is afraid of the questions or insecure enough not to reflect upon the answers. They certainly do not pretend knowledge, for if an answer defeats them, they must have the decency and confidence to say so, or else be unfit for the job. As for your quest, you should know enough to accept, reject or change the advice offered to you. Educating yourself to spot any gulf between presentation and content ensures that you are less likely to be fooled, or unintentionally fool others.

The imperative to lead

Thought—leaders become leaders by learning to lead themselves.

Individuals must lead themselves out of the unthinking world and into the conscious process of self-determination. Organisations must exercise leadership if the identity of the organisation and its products are to be successfully and profitably maintained.

Imagine that the leader of a large organisation realises that the organisation's identity needs to be seriously revised in order to secure its objectives and short-term survival. The rest of the management appear unconcerned or disagree on the grounds of time and funding. How should that leader ensure this issue is allocated a proper period of review and budget? They could use persuasion or compulsion.

A team comes to a halt through fear and superstition, yet one of the team knows the road ahead is clear. How should that member convince others to continue? They can try by attempting to lead by example.

The best leaders use a mix of persuasion, example and compulsion. Ideally, compulsion should remain in the background as a finality for those with whom other methods fail. For example, all businesses realise that to maintain cash flow is compulsory; failure to do so will be terminal. Likewise, the presence or implied presence of compulsion throughout an organisation is at times necessary for order and progress.

You should have, and be known to have, integrity, for it helps harness the loyalty and productivity of those being led. A personal touch is needed, regardless of your availability or remoteness—yet an awareness that it is more important to be recognised than to be popular. This involves enduring the potential penalties of unpopularity and isolation. You need to believe that your identity communicates the correct values, without much regard for the consequences. You must be prepared to defend your decisions and not shirk from the inevitabilities those decisions bring. This can mean being tenacious and determined enough to achieve, by force, and against opposition if necessary, yet remain flexible where circumstances dictate a change of approach, however abrupt it may seem, should change be necessary.

Finally, you need good overall judgement because the stronger your courage and determination, the more critical your application of judgement needs to be. By all means supplement that judgement by the judgement of those around you, but ultimately always listen most to your inner voice. The exercise of strong leadership without the balance of a penetrating mind is a potential catastrophe. Judgement is the team captain, fully informed, and conversant with all the fundamental issues, delegated or not.

The success of your identity, its communication and maintenance depends upon this ability to lead. It sets the altitude limit for what may be achieved. This height becomes the dimension and atmosphere within which your identity will be allowed to grow. Lower the ceiling height below what is required to satisfy your objectives, or the sensibilities or standards of your team, and you restrict your success directly.

Without the desire for excellence in leadership the best opportunities will be missed. Mediocrity of identity is a direct reflection of lack of leadership. In other words, the standard of your present and future identity is your fault before a design is even committed to paper! It is your responsibility of leadership already. Ah, the pleasures of being in charge...

Issues of leadership—external

The option to lead

Thought—the leader enjoys a clear track. Those following must accept the strains of following.

If you simply want to lead immediately, run your own race. You may elect to share the same track as others but the first race is now with yourself. Your own racetrack or not, determining your identity should be such a contest, not the senseless desire to chase others. By all means take an interest in their performance and make such comparisons as are useful, but set your own course rather than unquestioningly accepting others'. Who says they are right anyway? Perhaps they are following someone else too.

Thought—imitation is suicide.

It is if you want unique. And you need to engage the argument of how unique you wish to be. To imitate is to lose the potential of your own identity. Simply deciding not to copy and follow others produces the original—a difference which is yours alone. Some, unaware of their difference, do not necessarily understand the reactions they receive: they have yet to learn their advantage. And so the unfashionable or unaware-fashionable may live to rule the day; the unique through necessity become the invention, and the invention the difference the world was waiting for. The downside for some may include initial uncertainty, solitude, temporary or permanent unpopularity, but ultimately a notable identity, famous or infamous—if you have the time and budget for it to last in the long term.

The less than unique can draw reference or comfort from others in an effort to gain acceptance with the minimum of growing pains. They exist because of others: another who is creating or sustaining the market, or another whose patent has since expired. They do not plan to lead the market; they wish to follow. This is fine as long as you engage in the rules of fair play, and realise the limits you place upon yourself.

Original or alternative, genuine or insincere, your leadership determines the outer boundaries within which your identity will subside or grow.

Stop to go

Reflection

Before any difficult operation, you must prepare by stopping, sensing and reflecting upon your objectives. By attempting to probe these targets and the reasons for your motivation, you will find the task begins to take on some perspective.

Stopping is seldom a simple matter. It involves abandoning the responsibilities of the moment. Commitments will demand, with or without reason or concern for you, and their justification for interrupting your flow of thought, today, may have escaped challenge.

Thought—habits are convenient, but should convenience drive your identity?

Habits abound because of the convenience they offer—the benefit of repeating and therefore not needing to question your actions as closely as you might otherwise. Habits need auditing. But they'll do anything to avoid it. They hide with tremendous skill. It is as though they have a brain of their own. Which is the root of the problem: they dissuade certain parts of yours from exercising enough.

Start by asking how many times you repeat the same action or processes, yet hope, against all the odds, for a different result. How many of your actions and thoughts about the current organisation are mechanical by nature, rather than freely challenging? To halt the noise of the machine is to wake up to the silence you never realised surrounded you. WYSIWYG is not necessarily true. But finding out involves stopping, halting long enough to take a good look. It takes patience to stop, but halting now may not only increase your chances of achieving your aims, but speed the process up too.

Building or rebuilding an identity demands the inconvenience of construction. A need for a new identity may seem to be an urgent affair and the added strain of allocating a proper period for the workmanship to be completed may frustrate you further. It can seem overwhelming, for all aspects of the task seem to queue up for attention at once.

The wish of most leaders is to prove themselves with speed and alacrity. Ditto identity. But which race trophy you chase may have a bearing upon which race you enter. You may seek a finishing line, but where exactly is it, and for what reason is it worth crossing?

Objectives

Aiming anywhere in just a general direction is not only dangerous, but stupid. It is unlikely you will reach your target. Even if you do, how can you know, for you haven't verified where the target lies. It is absurd to start designing an identity in this way, yet this is exactly how most organisations proceed: sleepwalking across the firing range, distracted, impatient and unaware.

A vague sense of general direction, the wish to emulate the success of another, the blind pursuit of fame and fortune are all basic ingredients of ambition, and ingredients that do not set any clear objectives. Asking a design team to race away with no other information than this is, of course, folly. Yet both organisations and their designers being unable to prepare for true identity, beyond the courting of style minus substance, is a common phenomenon. Not my design team, you may be thinking... surely not on their fees... But how personally do you explore, and share, your vision? How often do you engage in abstract discussion with the one creative who improves you? What guidelines do you apply when designing any one component of your identity; and apart from the mechanical specifications, what summarises and controls your visual appearance?

Thought—style without deeper objective is zero substance.

There are an awful lot of applauded identities that, like paper ships slipping out of port, once on open seas blow or sink who knows where. This method of rudderless navigation means wasting costly resources, and begs the question: just how big is your budget? Worse, the audience misses the point of the exercise as soon as the press relations withdraw; but so will you and your workforce, for what confidence can you offer them? Your identity may be worse than useless, more negative than not trying at all. And when you end up eventually revamping it, you can add the cost of the refit to the original mistake. Assuming you get given a second chance.

If too little attention is paid to the dynamics of an organisation's identity, the early design work is unlikely to hit any known target. You might like the colour. The typeface may seem pleasing enough. A4 brochures with bland photography seem workable enough. Oh, and we'd better have smiling faces, use puns as much as possible, and a snappy 'strapline'. Now we're cooking...

No you're not. Cooking a weak stew with no body or sustenance perhaps. A diet of such identities and their promotion litters the world around you. They leave the audience feeling non-committal, because that is what they are: directionless.

When attempting a second design, without knowing the dynamics of the first, the difficulty of the process compounds. Repeatedly miss and your willpower will vanish, and a successful outcome become more unlikely with each successive attempt. Likewise, a design team on their second or third pitch lose their vitality. Clients drunk on endless presentations increasingly lose sight of reality too, and, should the unexpected solution appear during this stage, its acceptance or recognition by jaded minds cannot be guaranteed. In desperation, or to save face (or budget), an inappropriate solution may be adopted, or a cliché, if not a trend-hound fashionable one. Either way, you will no doubt have misconceived, with probably disastrous results.

Thought—tread carefully or stumble.

One, two, three: it is as easy as counting, yet simple enough to be missed by even the most able-minded. Let us be clear: treading carefully means one step must follow another; that the second relies totally on the first; that it can attempt to rectify a misplaced first step, but crucially, that it may not succeed. Next, number three has to build upon the success, or untangle the mess, of all that went before. Moral: withhold from commencing the design before you have prepared the way forward. Nothing that follows is more important than this first step.

Thought—you are searching for the one perfect identity.

Launching forwards with several ideas at once is reckless, unless the target area for the solution is clearly defined. You are seeking one solution—the correct, undisputed solution. One idea will stand head and shoulders above all the others. It is the one perfect idea. You can jump all around it or attempt to walk straight to it. Of course, working towards the single idea may not seem involved enough for those who are comforted by their own complications. They may want to see what they are missing. After all, they are paying for 'creativity'. But creativity should be employed fruitfully and to good purpose.

Even the most talented designers have only so many inspirational hours available to them when beginning a new project. This is the period when their inspiration rises to meet the challenge. Like you they only have so many hours in a day, so do you wish them to work steadily towards the best solution, or just scatter their time half-heartedly on alternative ideas (all the while thinking each one must be different), in the hope that one idea may spark some 'emotion' in you and your team?

There are times when to work on the fifty-seven alternatives will be the most productive and sensible course of action, but only when the purpose and direction of doing so is clearly understood. Or else all is so much grapeshot—undiscriminating and painful.

Thought—like true love, you'll know great identity when it hits you.

Failure to feel this strongly means you are off the scent, perhaps forever. You don't need to interview the world to find your true love. You have clues, shared values and recognisable traits. Concentrate and work with reason, and however insecure you may initially feel about employing a designer, involve them in this exploration. Be each other's psychiatrist if you must.

Never ask designers to 'pitch' without brief or fee. Even with payment never expect them to accept your brief without challenge. If the designer doesn't question your assessment of the situation (with verbal discussion or at least a defiant silence), think twice about employing them. You need to foster what should become an important relationship. Look for experts, but only those with the empathy and ability to inspire you. It sounds naive to some, but you must like them, and they you. You have a long and eventful trip to make—a shared set of objectives. You might as well enjoy the company.

Then there is energy, for without it you will not get very far. And unless you can demonstrate that you are capable of generating it, why should your workers, suppliers or customers provide the fuel?

Limitations

Thought—effective identity divides and rules.

An important role of an identity is to polarise the audience and act as a selection process for the classification of customer, supplier and prospective employee. In other words, it acts as a magnet, both attracting and repelling, however gently, through design.

A well-considered identity promotes efficiency and economy, both of action and expenditure. It enables improved communications, internally and externally, by offering a reason to examine and challenge the ineffectual, inefficient or obsolete. Yet when starting an identity programme the opposite may seem true: it may seem like expenditure with no immediate, tangible reward.

Other factors may also bar a new identity—but beware, for the same barriers can hinder all your objectives. They may include indifference or apathy within your team, age (too young to start, too old), market or geographical location (too close to see the opportunity, too far away to believe you can take advantage of it) and a shortage of self-knowledge and self-belief.

For some almost any belief is considered extreme, and therefore avoided or denied because of the risks that accompany the holding of it, actioning or revelation. The easy choice may appear to be not having any, but no beliefs equals a lesser identity and character, like a light bulb with no current.

Then there is that friend or more distant acquaintance: money. Just to talk of identity may sound expensive, even though the aim includes profile, profit and greater security. Often financial limitations are cited as the main barriers to an organisation's or product's success—the feeling that if only there was a larger budget, the expected miracle could be secured. But is money honestly the true culprit for under-achieving? True, it is an enabler, but lack of budget alone seldom stops those best deserving success. If necessary, at least be comforted that the rigour of economy works wonders for maximising the effectiveness of all you do. Economy tolerates fewer mistakes, whilst the luxury of waste can lead to many a downfall.

Thought—through incremental gain, grow yourself.

Yes, so you want the increments to be, well... bigger. But the point is that the fear of waste can, and certainly should, energise the powers of invention. What you can expect to achieve within budget is open to the negotiation which ingenuity offers us all. You have within you the choice and power of your direction and distance, and most of all the performance of your mind to excel regardless of any artificial barriers which attempt to contain you.

Steering

The need for guidance

An identity project needs firm guidance if it is to avoid hijack, unnecessary delay, partial or complete failure. This may sound a rather gloomy assessment, but the truth is that the introduction of a new identity often gives rise to much excitement and controversy. This excitement needs management if both supporters and challengers of the project are to be contained within the bounds of what you wish to achieve.

Discussing identity within the organisation releases energy. It should encourage managers and staff alike to express their thoughts and concerns. It can give vent to many previously unvoiced frustrations and much of this can take the form of criticism of the current management and the issue of the identity itself. Tolerate this as a small price to pay for people's involvement and enthusiasm. Not all their ideas will be sensible or logical, but listen carefully, for amongst these opinions are the roots of the current problem to be solved. You should accommodate this involvement without killing the project through committee. The way to do this is through a 'steering group'.

Internal resistance is to be expected and this can take many forms, from sulking and inwardly seething to outwardly aggressive, covert or head-on. Even though it may be limited to only a minor element, and perhaps easily controlled or rectified, you should be prepared for the added strain of having not only to plan the road ahead but also monitor all rear-view mirrors.

This is because a new order of substance may also be the arbiter of a more fundamental change of physical structure and attitude. An alert entrepreneur knows instantly that revising or developing a new identity is a potential catalyst for management change within an organisation that extends well beyond the obvious visual manifest-ations of graphic design. Before stepping into the ring it is wise to realise that reshaping an identity can often reshape the power struc-ture within an organisation in unexpected ways and at a surprising pace. If a newly planned identity poses all manner of shocking ques-tions, the answers may return a similar fire. Your sudden passion for probing questions, should it be untypical behaviour, may indeed be an uncomfortable experience for some.

The threat of fundamental change is a key problem for all organisa-tions, but especially for those which require a high level of trans-parency. For some a change of identity may need to be a democratic procedure, fully consulted and advised at all levels. Understandably they may need to fully involve and invite the opinions of their entire audience. For example, the change of identity for an organisation offering membership, partnership or allegiance to a common cause—and this covers a wide spectrum beyond just charitable organisations or clubs—may quickly become an emotional cyclone. Financial investors or emotional investors in an organisation, per-haps a loyal membership, benefactor or strategic partner, should be fully consulted, or they may be alienated from the start. But the flipside of consulting too much is that you may achieve less because of the possible compromises forced upon you, and the extended time which may be required. Here, as always, the success of the process is governed by the ability of the leadership.

For others less concerned about the consequences, a blitzkrieg may be the order of the day. And between these two extremes the politics of change can be managed in whichever manner increases the odds of excellence not being smothered by mediocrity.

Whatever the level of secrecy or openness the steering group must adhere to, it should intend to control the hub of the debate fully.

This group should ideally comprise no more than a dozen people, hopefully half that number. Regardless of whether you are an individual or the leader of a large organisation, you should include yourself and (assuming you are not also the designer) the design consultant, followed by a selection of other key personnel. Your management structure may determine the selection for you, though, in general, the fewer people involved the better. Do take great care with the politics of your selection for fear of alienating anybody of significant influence or opinion. There may be jealousy or suspicion from those you exclude, however astute your reasoning, and you should try to prevent any pointless bad feeling, which later on may frustrate the implementation of the final identity. Argument and differing opinions are valuable, so do not be afraid to include the dissenters, providing their intellect ensures mature discussion!

The design consultant must, of course, be an expert, but also someone comfortable and conversant at management level, lucid, articulate and not afraid to make enemies should reason demand it—a capable leader in other words. They may employ a team of other designers behind the scenes; that is not your direct concern, rather their ability to demonstrate clarity of thought and design. A major quantity of the much needed inspiration falls within their job description. Ideally, they should assume responsibility for running the group, providing your ego is able to make room for theirs. Indeed, it is often politically convenient to allow the designer this grace in order to remove any suggestion of bias within the group, in particular the accusation of any unfair influence over events from a particular faction within the management team. In doing so, you usefully transfer a good deal of the initial controversy and concerns onto the shoulders of an external and independent member of the group.

The purpose of this group is not endless meetings. You are busy enough as it is without having the time of your best management and yourself wasted by anything other than productive debate. Instead, the designer should convene the group only when critical to the process in hand. It is a forum for discussion and consensus designed to maintain the momentum required to successfully complete the project. The project can, and indeed should, challenge the present structure of marketing and communications within the organisation.

Another aspect of those you include within the group is that they should officially or unofficially represent different interested factions within the organisation. Some outside the group may feel more comfortable airing their views, in confidence or otherwise, with one particular member in preference to another. However, a member's inclusion in the group is also a matter of their contribution in terms of insight and expertise. If they are likely to attend meetings in a mute and ineffectual manner, do not include them! Your objective is productive debate, a gathering and radiation of the key issues throughout the organisation—not a lone motivator accompanied by a passive audience.

Allow the designer to interview all the members of the steering group, together with a selected cross-section of people outside this group, which may include suppliers and customers. The extent of this research depends upon the competence of the design consultant employed. You may need to supplement this information with more extensive market research. The larger the organisation, the more reassuring this becomes. But, ultimately, it will be the instincts of the design consultant together with the information supplied and agreement of the steering group that will decide the outcome.

Gathering opinion

Gathering the thoughts and opinions of others should include a series of one-to-one discussions, where you, the interviewer or interviewing panel, encourage discussion about the current, past and future of the identity in question.

Use a list of set points to be covered by the interviews but appear to be flexible and reasonably informal in your manner as well as in the order you approach these subjects. Avoid being rigid in your questioning or further discussion arising from answers you receive. Engender a relaxing atmosphere where the interviewee, unaware of the finer points to be covered, feels confident enough to share their experience, opinion and ideas without embarrassment or fear.

Should the conversation skip from one subject of interest to another, or fail to run in exact sequence, do not try to forcibly reorder it—instead allow the discussion to run its preferred course, remembering to return to all subjects to be covered before the interview is completed. You decide this conclusion. There is no set time limit. Some discussions may conceivably run into a number of hours, others only a few minutes. Remember that the survey is not a mindless brain dump but a selective process of enquiry. It is important that interviewees are made aware that they have the freedom, without recrimination or identification, to comment as they choose. Their vocalisation, however humble they may view their role or rank in the process or organisation, should be treated as both valid and effectual. You are inviting them to make their contribution towards the future of the whole organisation.

The list of discussion items should include the following:

- Background—an explanation of the history and events leading up to the current need for the identity project.

- Objectives—the currently perceived objectives.

- Opportunities—the currently perceived opportunities for the organisation, individual or product.

- Plans—the current plans to take advantage of or create the opportunities listed above in order to achieve the desired objectives.

- Barriers—the currently perceived barriers to progress, such as resources, cultural issues, the current identity, markets, competition and so on. Allow time for proper reflection, for many of these barriers are of an illusory nature. Pinpointing their exact position highlights not only the problems to be solved but the attitudes and character of both the interviewer and interviewee in terms of the existing predicament.

- Compulsory restrictions—what are the requirements of the law, finance and time?

- Client values—what values of the organisation do its clients seek?

- Your values—what values do you, the organisation or product offer in return? Concentrate not just on the obvious selling points but the often unspoken, unthought or intangible values. It is important to be persistent in your enquiries regarding this until you get some significant answers.

- Difference—what unique differences do you, the organisation or product bring to the marketplace?

- Price—what is the significance of price to the products and perceived image of the organisation?

- The current identity—discuss the negative and positive impact of any existing visual or written communications materials. This can include: actual products, case histories, publicity, building exterior and interiors, workshop facilities, uniform, vehicles or anything else viewed as a shared experience by employees, clients or the markets, local or remote, that you choose to or must operate within.

The results of this survey should not be a reiteration of the obvious, except where pertinent to the project before you. This is not primarily a survey of the physical or indisputable aspects of your past and present—though you ought to attempt, here or elsewhere, to summarise those concisely in order to focus them into a common reference point, or interpretation of history. Instead, this is an appraisal and subsequent mapping of all current attitude and opinion. You are searching for the organisation's intangibles.

As a general rule do not over-concern yourself with hard facts and figures. Use market research only where helpful in further highlighting the current state of corporate or audience mind.

This process of surveying stands every chance of tangling you in complexity, therefore your aim should be to remain semi-detached, though committed, and as far as possible an unfettered observer, looking only for the essence, deflecting all else in your path. You are searching for the cryptic or otherwise hidden, incomprehensible or abstruse issues. These threads are often finely spun and hidden within what is likely to present itself in the complex and possibly sophistical beliefs and frustrations of those interviewed. Until now no single person may have been in the position to fully see or grasp the opportunity.

The brief

Thought—a good brief is like a guided missile.

The guidance system should include a pattern of enquiry which allows you to cover the obvious factual aspects of what you need to know, as well as allowing you the opportunity to experiment and explore the more elusive issues which have arisen during the investigation and discussion of the survey. The brief should be a succinct document leading those who must use it to the most fruitful areas of thought and solution. The brief should act as the catalyst for enlightenment, and avoid being either unnecessarily rigid or verbose. It should communicate essence and act as intelligent guide for all. In this way it should close more avenues than it leaves open. And in doing so must limit in order to hit the target.

Some feel impatient to skip directly to the 'creative' work—to draw a picture or visual—but a good brief is the most fundamentally creative element of all. Later on, persistent failure in the design stage can often be rightly blamed on the weaknesses contained in the brief. Alternatively, you may not recognise the source of this confusion and, through pressure to move forward, agree upon a less than satisfactory solution.

An identity can also fail over a longer timeframe, even after launch. These failings may remain undetected for some time, perhaps not within the first twelve months of implementation. But you will gradually become aware of an ill-considered identity because it will be understood by you or others to be progressively ineffective. You may become increasingly uncomfortable or indifferent towards your identity. You may even become mildly embarrassed or offended by it. Where the internal or external dissatisfaction becomes severe, you may come under sustained pressure to withdraw or revamp.

In considering what is wrong, you will use every excuse other than the obvious: that the identity was flawed from day one. And the one you may therefore seek to replace it with will be likely to suffer the same fate, unless you regulate your impatience and do your groundwork. During which time, how much opportunity, credibility and advancement have you lost? Like the early years of an investment plan that stalls before maturity, you have paid dearly without receiving much interest. You have wasted your time and money, and owning up to this realisation will hurt.

Meanwhile a good identity builds from the brief upwards and needs no further justification. It justifies itself and flourishes with ease. A weak idea in presentation tends to demand excessive explanation or preamble. If a design team elects to present to you in just such a way, remain wary, with good reason.

Intangibles

Getting to know You

Thought—tell, boast or say nothing—but speak with care.

How can someone get to know about what you do and how well you do it? The answer is that they can know through the personal experience of meeting you or from what others say about you.

Alternatively they could ask you in person just how excellent you consider yourself to be, giving you the opportunity to answer as immodestly as you wish. Or you could tell them anyway, whether they have requested your opinion or not, by giving them a monologue on exactly how fantastic you believe you are.

Maybe you are too cautious to do either, which is wise, for there can be a fine line between telling and boasting. Worse, constantly telling others about yourself, regardless of their interest, quickly relegates you to the level of a self-centred bore. In this instance boring has little to do with repetition or consistency, which, in many situations connected to identity, is a positive force towards recognition and success. In contrast, boring somebody could be described as over-communicating that which needs no such emphasis. The solution is to realise the priority of the messages which need to be communicated and the best channels or methods for communicating them.

Thought—excellence is never boring.

Illustration 3

'Organisation A are the best'

by Independent Review

'Though I say it myself, I am the greatest'

Organisation A
Excellence guaranteed

There are many of ways of communicating the same message, yet in a subtly different manner. Create and choose the technique to suit your organisation or product.

Even for a dull personality there is a huge difference between appearing steady and uneventful, and boring an audience away. The former may be just what the audience wants, so they retain their interest, but a bored audience is one switched off by your message, dull or enlivening. You have lost them, assuming you found them in the first place.

For those destined or hell-bent on becoming an intriguing enigma, avoiding, censoring or being highly selective in exposing yourself from behind the mask of your planned identity—especially after achieving recognition through controversy or notoriety—can transform you into a powerful but elusive figment in other people's imaginations. This is a form of cult status. You restrict severely what you say, but allow your planned identity to say it all on your behalf. Refuse interviews, give one-word answers, act unpredictably, yet all the while the identity you elsewhere planned promotes you unashamedly, regardless of your contradictions, usually because of them.

Deliberately designed to be repetitive or not, a planned and co-ordinated identity improves and multiplies the opportunities to speak and the qualifications of what can be said. It is an opportunity to speak without speaking, boast without boasting. It communicates whether you are awake or asleep, there in person, speaking through a representative or have your lips selectively sealed. It endorses you, even though it is you endorsing yourself, for it works as though a third party. A loyal and tireless worker, it is a servant who quietly and relentlessly does what you ask of it and, subject to the abilities and limitations you specify when designing it, the servant you deserve. So before you start to construct your identity, you need to make certain you deserve what you seek. To achieve this requires a high level of self-understanding, and this means being self-rigorous. To deserve is to be owed a reward for effort. It is an exchange where the import of what you receive is in return for the export of what you gave. Take cheer from the fact that your return, all being well, will far outweigh your original effort.

1/3rd identity

Thought—your identity constitutes one third of your organisation's total effort towards success or failure.

The other two thirds are:

■ your products and services
■ your marketing and distribution.

When you examine this simple definition it may seem to be fundamentally obvious. Some may feel that perhaps this should have been stated at the beginning of this book. It is indeed a plausible introduction to the art of identity. But then again, perhaps not, because, despite its simplicity, it is too easily overlooked, and much too valuable to ignore. Too many organisations merely pay lip service to the role of identity. Even if they acknowledge or already benefit from the importance they give it, and of course many do not, most fail to realise the links between each third which comprises the effective whole. They settle for far less: an uncoordinated, partly functioning, untuned and unstable engine.

Like a triple-engine aircraft your organisation may be able to fly on two or perhaps one of its three engines, but less efficiently, with a higher cost in engine strain, maintenance and vibration. However, if each power source is precisely tuned and synchronised in order to perform together in harmony, the craft can be considered to be in trim, and maximum performance and safety assured. Result: a pilot in control, and the bonus of a safe journey.

The full benefits of a complete identity can only be achieved when each of these three sources shares the same objectives. They should all be contributing to and complementing the same ideals. They should certainly not be in conflict, or for that matter indifferent to one another.

Illustration 4

Identity

We stand for and promote the values of A, B and C.

Products and Services

Our products and services uphold and promote the values of A, B and C.

Marketing and Distribution

We choose marketing and distribution channels that promote the values of A, B and C.

Each third of your overall operation should confirm the position of the other two. To adopt any other position is a counter-productive waste of resources.

Objectives are usually factual by nature and often definable by data, for example sales targets, market share or physical size. Values are more difficult to communicate: you believe or say one thing, yet a fellow director or employee may believe and say another. Unless you can agree their definition, launching an identity with confidence, and then maintaining it afterwards, becomes a less than ideal process.

Body and mind

Accountants talk fashionably of 'tangible' and 'intangible'. They are increasingly of the opinion that the intangible may often be more valuable than the tangible, which is a problem for the unimagina- tive, for it means accounting for the unseen: goodwill, brand, inven- tion, patent and much more. Not that it should be a surprise to you: your mind is mostly intangible, your body mostly tangible. You can map your physical body a good deal more easily than you can map your mind.

So for tangible we can substitute the word 'body', and for intangible the word 'mind'. This is a useful word swop when considering your identity, its marketing and distribution.

The characteristics of the tangible are commonly agreed upon. They can be measured in units that others can also understand. But intangible is a matter of the invisible: the uncanny vision, sense or inspiration, and a lot more. These elements attempt to defy measurement or common agreement even amongst those respon- sible for their creation. For example, the entrepreneur creates suc- cess yet often has difficulty in explaining what exactly happened. The book-keeper asked to evaluate and rationalise this success must realise that they cannot fully explain either, except by the common units and protocols of their profession. Here, the only tangibles are those which clearly fit within these narrow definitions. Those who suspect a more expansive reality are left outside this consensus of measurement. Therefore the intangible remains an argument of conflicting estimation, its true value probably never officially agreed.

It often may fail to even be acknowledged by some. It all too readily escapes scrutiny.

It is easy to criticise, for the taking of measurements is not as easy as it may sound. Some things lend themselves to measurement more than others. For example, you can measure history, as it appears to exist in accountancy terms by quantity, date and fiscal depreciation. You can also measure physical body or land mass—we can all agree on the measurement of a measuring rule, whatever the system of units employed. Likewise we can produce an audit trail of name, products in stock, location and expanse of premises, transportation facilities, plant lists, the estimated size of the markets you target, the audited needs of the audiences via the statistics of market research, the market penetration in relation to the former, the overhead and profit of what you have achieved up until yesterday, and any other statistical information you stand a chance of gathering. This data is important and has value, but that does not mean that it should be accepted unchallenged, for data is an interpretation of apparent facts, and there will be faults due to the choices and limitations of accountancy procedure, and therefore interpretation.

Whatever the accuracy or interpretation of these tangible bodily statistics, they have less to do with the measure of mind—experience, characteristics of attitude, goodwill and future behaviour. This potential is guessed at, if estimated at all, as an extension of the known data. The potential for joy or despair that these intangibles may signify is seldom reflected with any confident accuracy on any annual account. Instead, they remain largely unaccounted for, or more usually, completely unknown. This is understandable, because these dynamics are elusive to the logic of arithmetic or traditional analysis. Whatever your summary of the intangible, it is most likely that you will have your sums wrong. For this reason many do not attempt to measure them at all, but they are misguided.

Within the computer age we have become used to using terms such as hardware and software. Because society has learnt to accept and agree the usage of these two words, we can now readily communicate their difference and implication. They have, over time, become tangible enough for them to be used in this debate, for it can be clearly stated that hardware is an identifiable mechanical or physical item, a body, large or discreet but obvious nonetheless. In contrast, the software, and its function, effect and potential value to the user, is far less easily defined. It exists in cyberspace, or call it what you will. Certainly a space which appears to defy physical boundaries. Yet software is a code or system written and therefore understandable by the human mind. As we did not author the human mind, we have a good deal more difficulty in understanding our own thoughts. Hence the ultimate intangible: the mind.

Your mind, our minds exist in a space and time unlike the more obvious physical world we appear to live within. We are both physical and emotional. Our bodies take up space, a space we can measure and agree upon, yet our imaginations escape all physical laws. Our thoughts fit within a framework which we have, over the centuries, struggled to build and understand. Concepts and theories only become tangible after consensus and, more usually, indisputable agreement. This agreement can take a long period of experience and post-rationalisation. The intangible may become at least semi-tangible as agreed by history. The intangible is the incomprehensible events of today, yet to be fully understood, yet to be agreed.

Valuing the 'mind' of an identity is acutely contentious. The cautious hesitate to agree with the more ambitious valuer, but all gamblers can at least find the comfort of common ground when agreeing tangibles. Therefore most data becomes a form of doomsday reporting; lust without intellect, the perverse priority to bodymap as though this particular body had not got a mind worth valuing. Such valuations account for body in historical and present terms, but cannot tell you who you are or the qualities which your audience attributes to you.

True, tangible data—and limited data of opinion that is gathered by survey—can indicate the possible future, help you anticipate the probable and react in advance to your estimates of public opinion, earnings or market pressures. It can help you to establish sales, cashflow and other data-led forecasts, but data alone does not and cannot tell you the complete story. It cannot truly measure the dynamic values, which your identity should be radiating, however hard it may try to do so. Unless we are more specific, no system on earth can measure quality, and indeed, arguably, no dictionary can give you a satisfactory or comprehensive explanation of the word. But it is within this battleground that fortunes are made or lost. You see what your rival cannot, then you worry as to whether their view may be more advantageous than yours. Events will finally tell you. Naturally, you would rather dictate the events.

Take a moment to contemplate Test 3 overleaf.

Test 3

Consider that you wish to produce and print a corporate brochure. Each of the two separate statements below summarises the sales pitch of two potential print suppliers and their identities.

Print supplier A

WE OFFER YOU THE LATEST TECHNOLOGY.

Print supplier B

We offer you our expertise.

Consider that supplier A is majoring on selling tangibles, whilst supplier B is promoting intangibles. The message to you is revealing in that it displays what they consider is the most important factor to both themselves and you, the potential customer.

For these suppliers either statement may be correct. It depends, of course, on how accurately they perceive their market.

Now, considering the presentation of your identity, contemplate the following:

- What category does your audience most value about your organisation —tangibles or intangibles?
- Which order of importance would you prefer them to be placed in?

To generalise and put it more bluntly, your identity and its presentation will offer one of the following three positions:

We offer you our character.

We offer you our statistics.

We offer you a combination of both.

Either a preference for tangibles, intangibles or an equal emphasis upon both is what your audience desires. Whether you elect to disagree or educate them otherwise, you would be advised to recognise their preferences. For some professions or organisations, the need to promote tangibles before intangibles will dominate. For example, your physical size, plant list, location, wealth, distribution, low prices or other attributes may be more compelling to your audience than attitudes, experience and values of character. Conversely, a list of tangibles may be much less important than you imagine, perhaps of no direct importance at all. So when telling an audience about yourself, don't make the mistake of getting these priorities wrong or you may only succeed in confusing, testing their patience or repelling them all together.

For example, it is not wise to spend the first three minutes of a five-minute presentation harping on about your geographical location and plant list if your listener is less interested in this (body) than your attitudes and level of service (mind). Likewise, avoid preaching about the quality of your mind when the punter is primarily interested in your body. You need not be entirely customer led—often customers need leading more in the interests of the long term than immediate gratification, but you do need to ask what speaks loudest for you—organisation or individual: your bodily specifications or your less visible qualities and characteristics.

Thought—effective identity is mind over body.

Whatever the importance of the static tangibles, your identity should be designed to accentuate your dynamics, for it is the 'mind' of your identity which ultimately supersedes any other reality. You need to explore this thoroughly enough to be able to recognise its valuable traits and promote them, or leave yourself exposed to the mercy of the unknown.

Recognition means the capability to manage, or else remain uncertain of creating and then maintaining an identity's direction and aim. Of course, the greater the distance your aim needs to travel and the more ambitious your objectives, the greater the need for a system of focus and calibration.

These dynamics are elusive of finite measurement, hence the endless debates about the true market worth of successful products and brands, yet they are the true destiny of an individual or organisation. They tend to endure, for better or worse. They create fortunes or destroy them. They instigate movement of desire or denial, action or inaction, advance or retreat. They are deeply rooted, usually by accident of birth or experience, and therefore difficult to identify, indeed often overlooked. How often do the successful fail to understand the underlying reasons for their success or the losers fail to remedy their fall from grace? And how often does the charismatic leader of an organisation become so entangled with the identity of their overall organisation or product identity that neither they, nor their audience, can manage to untangle the division between the two. Such a strong leader can, unless managed otherwise, become confused with the identity and habitual values of the organisation or product, because the intangibles of the leader are deliberately used, or accidentally allowed, to dominate the intangibles of their organisation or product.

Unless you attempt to define the intangible mind which underwrites your visual identity you cannot manage or measure its relevance, effectiveness and application.

Further, if you cannot identify how these dynamics present themselves or appear visually to those who view you, you cannot knowingly lay your foundations. And if you cannot be certain of the foundations, you have serious cause to be apprehensive about the strength and stability of the structure you are intending to build upon them. Hence the need to map the ground you wish to stand upon. This takes insight and perseverance, but the reward is a certainty that will thereafter save much wasted effort and inappropriate or unnecessary risk.

Foundations

Identifiable position

All effective identity starts from an identifiable position. It is like a framework or building constructed within the minds of those who encounter it and, in the same manner as any physical structure, it grows within the potential weight limits that its foundations are able to accommodate and thereafter maintain.

If you tire of the need to concentrate upon the foundations it may be because their purpose is normally to remain unseen or unspoken of, which is fine, because their job is to underpin what we see on the surface, not to boast about their own existence.

It all too commonly surprises some to suddenly realise that they must budget for and produce adequate support. Instead of building upwards, you now find yourself digging downwards—and only to refill the holes later. This may test your nerve and patience: time appears to be against you (when isn't it?) and digging is not as showy or obviously satisfying as seeing the eventual construction rise before you. Meanwhile you may have the continual pressure of those people who must or simply cannot help themselves from peering over your shoulder. Added to which, before the earthmovers begin there may be a large amount of dangerous, awkward and sensitive demolition work to complete. These inconveniences must be negotiated before construction can begin. Alternatively, you may have started the building of your structure long ago, or inherited it in the current state of repair. Whether a complete rebuild is necessary or not, you benefit from revisiting the integrity of the foundations.

Before investing time and money in the pursuit of a new or improved identity, it is worthwhile contemplating how you will measure the relevance, effectiveness and accuracy of the work you are about to commence. This identity may eventually be applied to many forms of communication materials and events. Therefore a method of debate, selection and appraisal of these visual manifest-ations would seem to be not only invaluable but essential.

When architects plan structures they begin by studying the survey and questioning the original request. Taking into consideration the objectives of the client, they start to design accordingly. They must calculate the nature of the supporting structure or terrain. The greater the size of the new structure, or the less supportive the underlying surface, the greater their requirement. The purpose of this preparatory work is not to be wasteful, but purposeful. It is in anticipation of what is to follow. The foundations serve the structure for as long as it needs to remain standing safely.

Skyscraper or tent?

The foundations of the former need to support extreme weight. That much seems obvious. You may wonder how anything so large can stand so firmly rooted. The latter, like any temporary structure, perhaps an exhibition stand, appears at first glance to have a mini-mal requirement. But on second thoughts, if the tent is one compo-nent of a much larger operation, and your overall target is still the stars, the collective organisation will still demand the skyscraper foundations. Of course a tent is portable, but its visual foundations should remain tuned to those of your core identity (your base camp or HQ) or if you are a perpetual traveller, the strength of your back.

And how strong is your back? The location and building of found-ations is hard work. Spade or mechanical digger, it is not for the impatient or those afraid to question themselves and others. The search is for the inherent or appropriate materials that will be able to take the burden of weight and responsibility—and beyond just the initial launch period. The sooner you start, the better. Pity those

Illustration 5

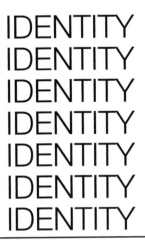

IDENTITY
IDENTITY
IDENTITY
IDENTITY
IDENTITY
IDENTITY
IDENTITY

SUPPORTING SUPPORTING SUPPORTING SUPPORTING
INTANGIBLES

The horizontal line is ground level.

What supports the visible must be of suitable strength.

who reach the first floor only to realise the foundations below now limit the growth they wanted beyond, so the penthouse they desired to occupy cannot be as high as once hoped. Or worse, they believed they were successfully on their way to Floor 101 only to find, on constructing the first staircase, that the team in charge of calculating the depth and strength of the foundations believed it was to be a bungalow.

Thought—if we must build on sand, let us know its quality.

Your first unavoidable dilemma is to realise that it is the intangibles which are your foundations. All but the most inventive or confident wantonly deny this truth. Identifying and managing these becomes the foremost need of any truly worthwhile and sustainable identity. Ignore or dispute this truth and your identity is doomed to obscurity or dire failure. Engage in the argument to identify them as far as you are able to, or struggle without a paddle.

Identifying intangibles requires a discussion. This means, for many, an uncomfortable level of abstraction. You have a need to identify what others may either not be able to see or not wish to risk being seen to see for fear of being foolish. The struggle to grasp what for many seems the unreachable takes you outside and beyond the normal confines of logic. Deny the validity of labelling these dynamics or not, we all are subject to them. Recall the tests in the introduction to this book and our tendency to make emotional judgements beyond any conscious reason.

These intangibles, your intangibles, need to be labelled. The only method at our disposal is in our choice of descriptive words which may help us judge both the intangibles themselves and the suitability of the elements of your overall visual identity that are based upon them.

The need is for words that will not break too easily under the weight of inspection, words that inform and confer an acute or intense visual meaning. These words must pinpoint when your identity is

Illustration 6

unfocused identity	unfocused identity
consensus of identity through both structured and unstructured discussion with external consultants and differing levels of internal management on a project-by-project basis: ad hoc or improvised identity management	**consensus of identity through the agreed use and debate of identifiable foundations and intangibles:** firmwords
unfocused identity	focused identity

Choose your method of identity management, and therefore focus.

working at the peak of its focus and potentiality. Not vagaries such as 'quality' or clichés such as 'leading edge'. These words are too blunt or weak in substance and liable to misunderstanding or the arguments of fashion; such words are breakable in that they dissolve, fragment or subside, leaving behind words that offer more visual clarity, character, resonance and durability. You need words of substance that will support weight and stress, concrete words that are capable of working tirelessly beneath the surface of your identity. For this reason, and because it is useful to refer to these words by name, they are called *firmwords*.

Measurement

The need to measure

Thought—any fool can attempt to measure, but who can measure identity?

Without a system of value recognition, an identity can and will easily fall into disarray because it cannot be effectively managed or measured. An identity does not stand still. It cannot. It is active, growing by incremental gain and loss each day. It reacts and responds to the changes it must endure. It is both diminished and added to daily by the events and people who feed and support it, as well as those who draw sustenance from or possibly even attack it.

Disregarding the audiences outside the organisation, within it you may share common values and opinions about the desired identity, but unless the essence of those values can be translated and agreed readily, and with rapid consistency, the focus of the identity is likely to stray.

Thought—an identity should be a zone of zero waste.

There should be no wasted effort or needless expenditure of energy. Everything which constitutes or represents the identity should exist for a positive reason justifiable by firmword.

For example, your management, staff or agency may, by the nature of their ignorance or misinterpretation, contradict the intangibles upon which the identity is founded. And when presenting their vision for your identity—perhaps a new uniform or corporate brochure—what process of reasoning will you employ to measure the visual appearance and content of their ideas? These ideas are threatening to add or detract from your identity. Unless you rigorously challenge their inclusion, with a consistent method of approval or rejection, you abdicate control.

Identity is not simply a matter of style—like or dislike—for style alone is only an embellishment, or passing fashion. The intangibles denoted by firmwords are the ultimate foundations of an identity, and their maintenance should not be compromised. Their unerring truth is their strength and beauty. Therefore any aesthetic decisions should be made in direct relation to these values.

If you fully realise these visual codes, you can provide quick and incisive reasoning when judging any visual manifestation, from correct brochure design to correct clothing, from correct colour to correct shape.

So what words should be your firmwords? How can you find and describe in just a few single words that which denotes your identity?

Consider a possible firmword, 'interactive'. As an example only, could the medium of communication and elements with which this identity is promoting itself be justified by their application? Does the effect of such random elements as headlines, photographs and illustrations agree with, support and further clarify the meaning of this firmword, or do they contradict? Perhaps these elements neither imply, suggest nor overtly state conformity or denial of this firmword, neither confirming nor refuting, registering nor suggesting any connection, however tenuous, with 'interactive'. If so, the next and most obvious question is why are they being used at all? At best they may add nothing to the identity as indicated and measured by this single firmword. At worst they may detract, confuse or simply be a series of meaningless statements. If so, omitting them would be more advantageous than continuing to fund their use.

Of course, the precise relevance and rationale of a firmword depends upon the nature of the organisation or product it is intended to represent. For example, imagine that in this particular example, the firmword 'interactive' represents the notion of enabling users to communicate both into and out of an imaginary centre, regardless of geography, social or professional standing. It may represent reciprocality; to act on each other; to behave in a way that influences and responds to one another; a two-way flow of information, responding to input from the users and suppliers alike. 'Inter' could be interpreted as meaning amid; between; among; source; enter. 'Active' could be understood as given to action rather than speculation; practical; originating and communicating; working; effective; alive; and capable of modifying its state or characteristics in response to input or feedback. These details, the rationale behind a firmword, must be sufficiently established because they are the roots that support and provide the forum for all subsequent discussion and interpretation of the firmword they explain. Establish and know them well and the endless connections they promise to provide will advance a mastery of identity unavailable by other means.

These values should describe the combined effects of your visible identity. They are the vital messages and general style that your identity radiates, as created by your use of typefaces, photographs and illustrations. Their overall effect should be to convey and contain a worthy depth of meaning, which can stand debate within your own mind, as well as those in your immediate team. They should, within the realms of what must be a necessary abstraction, be wholly relevant to both you and your customers' needs, as well as being an active and simple recipe for creative decision-making and evaluation. Get it right and there is a big reward: design certainty.

Design certainty

Choosing and then using the firmwords with which an identity should communicate should be a priority. Internal management and marketing, as well as external designers or promoters, benefit from knowledge of what makes a justifiable, relevant and valuable contribution to the identity. This means an agreed understanding of the values chosen to represent the identity. The necessary discussion will promote a process of partnership, knowledge and commitment, and give force and direction to all subsequent opinions from both parties, however weak or irrational those opinions may at first appear.

The agreement of what goes into the foundations provides the rationale for all future discussions of this nature. What is considered to be correct or incorrect, in general terms or detail, will thereafter promote significant savings in deadline, anxiety and budget. The client stakes an ownership, understanding and involvement in their own identity, whilst the external designer, sharing the same agreement about the nature of the identity's foundations, can unhesitatingly unleash their creativity and commitment of time with a focus and confidence impossible to achieve by any other means. Complete knowledge of these values is far more likely to provide apt and exciting results than a designer fearful of a client's reactions to any given design approach or interpretation of brief. It is less worrying for the client too, because each presentation now has a basis of judgement to which all parties have agreed; uninformed like and dislike become irrelevant, and positive or negative criticism becomes focused and more easily articulated than before. All becomes buttressed by a keen knowledge of the foundations being built upon. The designer can continue to challenge the client's understanding of what these foundations will bear, and the client actively participate in debating the design solutions being recommended.

Firmwords

As an individual or organisation, can you unhesitatingly explain what you do and the values that you believe in? If the answers are not easy, why not spend a while interviewing yourself! You should have done this during the survey period when you gathered your thoughts and the thoughts of other interested parties. Look back at these notes afresh and spend some time further reflecting upon your findings. Develop some answers that are not only sincere and descriptive but, in your opinion, are appealing to both you and your target audience. The values you are seeking should form a two-way mirror: that is, they should represent the fundamental strengths of your product or service as well as being the chief motivators in the eyes and ears of your target audience.

They are words which are primarily capable of lending themselves to visual interpretation: they can be represented, conveyed and understood through the medium of pictures. Certainly a single picture should be capable of conveying the prime meaning of the intended firmword, although, if you are depending upon an audience consciously (rather than unconsciously) comprehending or linking this picture to this particular word, it may almost certainly require the addition of some simple verbal or written qualification. This would also be true of almost any picture used within the confines of an advertisement or other promotion, for seldom can a picture alone be used without a headline or other qualifying statement to make its purpose clear. (If it can, it is an icon, with a power beyond words, however many we may try and attribute to it.) The point is that the underlying statement of the picture should conform to, or indeed promote, the word being concentrated upon. More importantly, and of much greater significance, beyond this single and probably simple representative picture, the expert designer (a trained and visually literate person) can and should utilise the same word and meaning with varying degrees of subtlety or abstraction, so that all graphics such as layout, pictures and choice of typefaces, as well as all issues of format, headline and text matter, permeate with the same general meaning. Firmwords are words which justify your existence as well as your message or communication. If you cannot justify an action or item of communication in relation to them, do not include them as part of your identity.

Thought—no action is better than inappropriate action.

Test 4

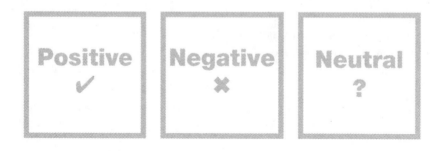

To narrow down or formulate your firmwords, make three pin boards or desk surfaces under the three headings above.

Select and pin up all current visual manifestations of your identity onto one of the three pin boards depending upon how you feel about them. Any item you feel uncertain about or do not identify strongly with as being either Positive or Negative must therefore be Neutral.

When judging any object such as buildings, vehicles, purpose-made exhibition stands, gift items, clothing or any other structures or methods of physical communication

make selections on the basis of
purpose—shape—format—size—weight—texture—colour

When judging actual content

make selections on the basis of
typeface—photograph—illustration—subject matter—word/phraseology
—space—layout—colour

Every visual aspect of your identity should justify its inclusion or continued existence by comparison with these words. This covers all aspects of visual identity and activity—to the most extreme levels of application. To assist you in your quest to find these words, you need to look at as many of the current manifestations of your identity as possible. Study your current usage of colours, typefaces, printed items, signage, photographic material, clothing, accessories and interiors with an eye to which strikes you as effective, and therefore appears to add value to your identity, and which is neutral or appears to detract from your identity.

Firstly, look for items which strike a major chord either in your heart or the hearts of others. These items may appear to be instinctively correct for the identity in question. They could be said to speak in a louder, more confident voice than the other items which surround them, as well as tending to increase the effectiveness of identity and your morale. Perhaps these items have already proven their effectiveness, and maybe this is already reflected in some measured increase in sales or market effectiveness. Also, perhaps a particular leaflet design, typeface or photograph appears, though you may not necessarily know why, to epitomise the ethos of the organisation or product being surveyed. Meanwhile other manifestations of your existing identity may only cause minor excitement, or none at all. Perhaps some may go as far as to embarrass or repel you. Other items may appear to be ineffectual or obstructive to the aims and objectives of the identity.

This process does not mean reacting only to standards of workmanship, or quality of printing but accounting for visual impression and empathy—you are searching for those items that improve you, deny you or appear to do neither.

You may take your time and change your mind several times as you start to enter into this thought process. Your casual opinions should soon develop into the beginnings of a reasoned classification and understanding of what reflects your organisation in the best light.

Do not be alarmed if most of the items appear within the negative category or if, at this stage, you are not sure of the exact reasons for their initial selection. Notice that some items may contain contradictory elements; for example, you may feel a particular colour on a brochure is positive, even though the subject or style of an illustration appears to be negative.

Continue to make these judgements even if unsure of your reasoning. Follow your instincts. Trust yourself! If you are short of elements to judge, complement by adding others. Borrow images or items from elsewhere, such as the brochures of others, advertising you have noticed and been attracted towards or magazine cuttings in general.

This process is defining patterns and profile. With the positive items only, gradually attempt to clarify your reasoning for each selection and the common denominators they share. Start to understand these common values and jot down randomly the words that best describe them as they occur to you.

However unconvincing or baffling you find the beginnings of this process, group these words into general areas of value. You may start to define several areas of concentration. If so, continue to puzzle the commonality between the words you are writing down in an effort to reduce or expand the number of areas into three distinct groupings. By striving for three groups of words you will ensure that your thoughts and the words themselves will receive most thorough scrutiny.

Again, however difficult a task it may seem, reduce each group of words to just a single word. The aim is to distil your selection down to just a single word from each group—making three words in total. Yet again, this inevitably forces you to work extremely hard in justifying your selection.

To assist you further, make full use of a dictionary, thesaurus, synonyms and antonyms, or any other vocabulary tool. In particular, once you start to feel confident about a certain word, search for and compare other words of a similar meaning which perhaps offer slightly more energy or definition. There may be several words fighting for the same position; allow time to prioritise them in order of effectiveness.

The interaction between these words should provide a further dynamic which none of the words acting individually is capable of achieving. Verify your selection by asking if each word accurately and steadily describes an element of what you and your organisation possess. Is it an authentic and (as far as possible) unique intangible that you offer? Does it also appear to be upheld in the opinions or desires of your audience? Are you are also confident of providing, defending and proceeding with this concept as part of your strategy for the foreseeable future? In other words, is each word justifiable?

The words you are searching for need to relate to the visual aspects of your identity—both picture and word. Continue to authenticate them against the items previously considered as adding to your identity. They should confirm or explain why these images appear to work so well. Also test the words by applying them against the more obtuse visual manifestations or decisions relating to your identity, such as office furniture, automobiles and personal clothing. Reflect upon which charities or sponsorship events this selection of firmwords would make your organisation compatible with.

Being drawn from different groups, each word should promote a separate meaning and usage, lending them each to a distinct visual interpretation. What is visually exploitable may be seen more readily by some, unappreciated by others. You need to be visually literate, or include a member in your team who can provide this insight. Ideally the designer you employ should be able to combine both visual and verbal insight, for it is this articulation of the gulf which often divides the two that is necessary if you are to fully realise and understand. Work together until you both understand the rationale of the firmwords. If they are imperfect, they are misleading and therefore inappropriate or possibly dangerous to use, so proceed with care. The upshot is that all members of your steering group should be able to understand and begin to articulate their application. When you are satisfied with your final selection, the words can be worthy of being called firmwords. 'Firm' because they represent the immovable foundations of your current identity.

Illustration 7

Here the same underlying word helps to support the other words and phrases—it is, in effect, their possible common denominator.

well-engineered

durable

thorough workmanship and materials

durable

traditional values

durable

When thinking about your own identity, work until you have found such a word capable of describing and supporting all others which would otherwise pretend to describe this one area of intangibles. In this example, 'durable' would appear to be suitable, and is a descriptive word capable of being translated and understood in both photographic images and attitude of word, speech and other presentation.

The result should be a visual definition of how your identity should be focused on both yourself and your audience.

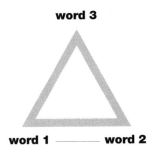

The final selection should ideally provide two words (words 1 and 2), which complement each other, but perhaps with some element of tension between them. It might seem as though these words have some contradictory effect upon each other. The third word (word 3) may appear to stand apart and infer a tendency to reconcile the tension between the other two, probably by offering reason, direction and leadership to the difficulties or tension created by them.

These words become the mixture with which you will promote and measure the effectiveness of your identity. They may not directly refer to your literal business activity or product, indeed that is unlikely to be helpful. Instead, they are a combination that together create a real difference—your difference—the difference between you and your competition. They establish a code for what is fully justifiable and in accordance with your identity and what, however professional or attractive, is not. This process is not to be confused with mission statements or phrases that explain the obvious. Firmwords describe the base workings of your values—not bland reiterations of the common values of others.

The following test illustrates some sample firmword combinations and how they can be applied:

Test 5

Below are some sample combinations of firmwords.
(word 1—word 2 : word 3)

- **geometry—art : active**

- **alone—communion : reprise**

- **change—secure : forever**

- **solo—family : happiness**

- **simple—intelligent : enlightening**

- **minimum—maximum : leading**

- **independence—teamwork : co-ordination**

Each firmword combination can be applied to an individual, organisation, product or service.

Match each combination to one organisation, individual or product from the following list:

- **technical author**

- **network printers**

- **computer software**

- **fashion house**

- **cigarettes**

- outdoor clothing

- internet service provider

- restaurant chain

- management consultant

- perfume

- stockbroker

- pop star

- laboratory equipment

- ...this book

Firmwords form the foundation for endless creativity—all within the boundaries of what fits and summarises your visual identity. Together they form a unit of multiplicity that will maintain focus and provide the most direct route towards the expansion of your identity within the minds of your audience.

Notice how unexpected and refreshing these combinations can prove when experimented with or swopped between one organisation/product and another. They all offer a system for developing and managing the dynamics of the article being represented.

Of course the definitions of each individual word and combination are personal to the organisation or product they belong to. Their precise meaning and justification may and should be known only to them. Unless you are fully versed in their character and management objectives, how else can you readily interpret their peculiar meaning and inference?

What is clear is that you should develop a short, written rationale for each word and, in addition, the combined group of words as a whole, so that the interpretation and representation of the words can be further communicated, supported and explored as necessary.

Using firmwords

There is no limit to the usefulness of these firmwords. Combinations and subsets can be devised and employed to suit the complexity and depth of your identity. If chosen wisely, your firmwords are a simple and powerful reckoning tool for measuring the performance of your identity—or for that matter, any article of communication which operates under the guises of your identity. Certainly use them when judging the effectiveness and relevance of such items as a logo, brochure, typeface, photograph, illustration, advertising campaign or office interior. Gauge the validity of the concept and design by comparing them with your firmwords. An item may satisfy one or two of the three words, but does it satisfy all three?

Test 6

Consider the firmwords of minimum—maximum : leading.

Without any other knowledge, contemplate what would be a suitable activity to sponsor from the list below:

motor-racing

croquet

golf

local school charity run

cricket

squash

bar billiards

tug of war contest

beauty contest

national televised song contest

marathon running

hunting event

nature reserve

drugs awareness campaign

London to Sydney solo flight

Which activity satisfies as many of the three words as possible?
Shun any which contradict any one firmword.

The quality and nature of the activities being organised and promoted, including those of the organiser, are both important influences. Start to eliminate, with harsh judgement, the subjects appearing to contradict, or not fully or obviously satisfy, the notion of leadership. Some of the team games do include an element of leadership, but some focus upon a clearly defined leader more than others. The subjects also need to satisfy the notions of 'minimum' and 'maximum', so fail when compared with some of the others. 'Minimum' seems to infer distillation: the least possible, reduction, size or duration, certainly not waste or unnecessary luxury. 'Maximum' likewise seems to infer a certain rejection of compromise, as well as a full response, but also contradicts the word 'minimum' in suggestion of duration or size. 'Leadership' reconciles the other two words in that it can lead to both extremes, and often a worthy contention or combination of both.

For example, motor and cycle racing appear to offer both minimum and maximum—a power-to-weight ratio which strives for minimum weight and for maximum performance. Both produce leaders. Providing you are likely to be seen to support the eventual leader or facilitate the tournament, thereby making the selection of a leader possible, these would seem suitable.

The London to Sydney solo flight fails to provide a leader unless it contains an element which makes possible the breaking of a world record or other physical or spiritual barrier. Perhaps the aviator is already an established figure who represents leadership for other reasons. And so the arguments can continue. The important point is that the debate is purposeful and focused upon what is correct for this particular identity. By establishing the incorrect so rapidly, we save unnecessary effort and expense, as well as protecting the identity by measurement and matching of values.

Through this trial and error of discussion you will gain an insight into what works for your identity and what, though professionally presented and not unappealing, is counter-productive or failing it. One of this technique's most instant rewards is the identification of the missing ingredient—a design is almost acceptable, yet 'something' is missing. Your firmwords should quickly prompt the correct answer.

As stated clearly elsewhere in this book, there is a distinct liberation in concentrating upon what is correct and dispensing with all other effort. From now on you can repeat your aim with deadly accuracy. You can relax in the knowledge that all you do is promoting your identity in the direction you plan. This certainty of focus may significantly alter your attitudes to investment of time, money and other resources in general, impacting beyond the one third of your operation which is considered to be the domain of your identity alone. You can prioritise with a new alacrity and purpose, confident of your actions. What you now change, avoid or refuse will free you for the new opportunities before you.

Thought—single-mindedness propels a clearly defined identity.

Examining fake intangibles

A fake intangible is the insincere or thoughtless use of signals or items that pretend to represent something the wearer does not fully intend, believe in or match with their own ability, intellect or moral intention.

If a hotel places a bust of Nero in its reception hall, it ought to know why, as a symbol or decoration, it is being used. Insincerity can be interpreted as foolish or insulting. In contrast, sincerity demands self-awareness and discipline—qualities prompted by proper adherence to firmwords.

The true and inherent are earned. You cannot simply copy the perceived intangibles of another and remain convincing. You need to experience your own truth through the labours of your own devotion. The spade before you cannot easily be handed to another.

Having successfully got this far, you can now proceed to plan the structure of your identity. What you build will be in accordance with the nature and strength of the firmwords. There are further decisions to make, but now the rewards for your early efforts will start to pay dividends.

Consistency

Identifiable mass

The binding element of all identity is consistency, for if there is no consistency there is no conformity, and if there is no conformity there is no identifiable mass.

Apart from sounding complex, this may appear to be a contradiction, for conformity can amount to camouflage. In other words, your identity becomes lost amongst the mass you choose to camouflage yourself within. In this instance, and regardless of whether you are conscious enough to notice it, what you believe to be your consistency in fact belongs to another. You merely elected to copy another or group of others, and in doing so became merged with their broader or collective identity.

Thought—you should ask yourself whether your identity belongs to you, your direct competition or the identifiable mass of your perceived market area.

It is easy to lose definition of identity in this manner. Your identity needs critical mass. An audience needs to be able to clearly recognise your sameness, but not necessarily because this sameness is a consistency also shared by your competitors, for that is merely conformity with others. You certainly require conformity with yourself; a trueness of self; a consistency of self. Where this conformity also spills into representing conformity with the competition is another matter for you to decide upon.

Consistency creates something far more powerful than most realise: this is predictability. The presence of predictability is vital if you are to create trust, and in return trust creates an outcome that both you and the audience can mutually benefit from. Of course what we trust can be consistently either good or bad. You can be trusted to be consistently either. The important point is that trust is the fabulous by-product of consistency. If your identity lacks predictability it must therefore be inconsistent. If you are inconsistent you succeed in communicating potential confusion and therefore the possibility of distrust.

Consistency by itself does not guarantee that your audience will have a favourable opinion of you but, as a result of what they believe to be your consistency, they will have identified you. This can be excellent if it results from planning, but ultimately unhealthy if by default. Beware that although the unplanned can produce acci-dental success, it can just as accidentally be destroyed.

Consistency is often the invisible force which underlies an identity. Yet surprisingly it is frequently abused and mismanaged by those who fail to understand its true value. Often the owner of a successful identity will damage that same success through a lack of under-standing: they fail to comprehend the nature and importance of their consistency and therefore allow it to fracture, weaken or break irreparably. Just like a reputation, consistency can always stand improvement, but it is much harder to repair once damaged, and often broken beyond repair.

Do not be surprised to find that the realisation of consistency plays such a crucial role in all our day-to-day decision making. We con-sciously or unconsciously seek confirmation through the recognition of patterns. There is a need to recognise patterns. With patterns we can more confidently predict. The more pronounced the patterns we note, whether or not we fully understand their import, the more secure we will feel about the decisions being made. It just might be your sixth sense, because whether you believe in the existence of a sixth sense or not you are nonetheless forced to use your skills of prediction whenever you must decide between products, services, organisations or individuals. You may be deciding upon a new car; a charity to make a donation to; a gas station to refill your fuel tank; an airline to fly with; a job offer to a prospective employee; a new career move; a church to attend; a marriage partner—you name it.

Your criteria for these decisions are based upon the performance you seek versus the pattern of performance you detect. Detection includes the recommendations of others, publicity and advertising campaigns (including those you thought you couldn't remember) and your direct experience (regardless of limitations) with the subject you are compelled to judge. You scan for information to satisfy your desired level of trust and predictability. The core of this examination is based upon the demand for consistency.

The underlying strength of all identities, your identity, depends upon this consistency. Long or short term, your audience will gauge you on this pattern and performance. Your values may not be the same as theirs—indeed, they may neither recognise nor agree with your values—or not yet. Perhaps you may even hope as much. Maybe by the time others finally recognise your objectives you may have already long left the market; or perhaps emerged as the leader you always knew you were...

To what extent do you find a purchasing decision hard work? The answer may depend upon the subject matter, for this may determine your interest. Some subjects hypnotise more than others. Perhaps you shy away from detail or perhaps you revel in it. Either way, notice how you automatically become engaged in forming a decision based upon the recognition of a pattern that suits your need, and patience.

It takes concentration to remain still long enough for others to identify your position, or for you to study theirs. Perhaps, like me, your ability to concentrate is often selective, fickle, sometimes inattentive or just plain lazy.

The first pattern to be perceived and accepted (the first impression) may prove conclusive for some; subsequent patterns which become revealed later either confirm the first pattern or contradict. Confirmation breeds trust, contradiction breeds yet more confusion.

Thought—what opinion do you form of individuals who seem to contradict themselves by inconsistent behaviour, dress or appearance?

Whatever the identity being viewed, recognising a pattern depends upon spotting the pattern repeat. No repeat and the design appears to be random. In other words, it remains unknown or unpredictable because there is no element that we can be certain will be repeated. We may find ourselves making judgements on the slimmest of evidence. Perhaps the item, individual or organisation is new to you. You simply do not have enough information to make any accurate appraisal of their consistency. Yet the urgency to do so may be impossible to resist. Regardless of any firm information available, if the identity on view is offering the right manner and level of visual consistency, you will most likely be satisfied.

Thought—failure to recognise a pattern promotes insecurity, whilst recognition is comforting.

You might also like to reflect on how clothed in secrecy you or your organisation appear to those inside or outside. Even if the world reads your advertisements, does your identity remain a barrier to greater understanding? Is your consistency unmistakable? Do your players know what team they are playing in? Does the centre forward know who the left back is? And anyway, where's the football? Why are you passing me a baseball? And he thinks its cricket.

The sophistication of the pattern determines the ease with which it is identified. This defines the target audience: the easier the pattern, the larger the catchment area. Likewise, the more sophisticated the pattern, the more it may act as a barrier—admitting only a more select audience—or, if coded sufficiently, a secret organisation.

Thought—how many organisations do you encounter which alienate you with either too much sophistication or too little?

Sophistication of pattern is no pattern if the audience is unable to see it. Too easy, too hard, the visual patterns you construct in the minds of the audience operate the barriers and doorways to the content your identity may promise. To a major extent this determines your accessibility and eventual audience, depending upon that audience's desire or definition of sophistication. One audience, or section of an audience, may find a simple pattern off-putting, perhaps even crude. Another audience may find a simplistic pattern, especially a deliberately simplified one, not just easily understandable, but perhaps even suggestive of an equality they positively wish to associate themselves with—and be seen to associate with. In such ways the pattern complexity of an identity versus the sensibilities of the audience have a lot to do with inclusion or exclusion.

A pattern too dense or complex may threaten if perceived as a social code by a section of the audience who may as a result feel unconfident or unable to understand the subtleties of the presentation before them. Through fear or prejudice they may retreat before you. Perhaps this is a useful idea. If not, think again, for like the language and complexity of the vocabulary you use to speak with, you must also carefully consider the signals you send towards the eyes of those who see you.

Test 7 • sophistication of pattern

This test is the comparison of two illustrated patterns:

■ **Pattern 1**—a simple pattern that creates a simple certainty.
  It is easily understood with only a small area visible.

■ **Pattern 2**—a more complex pattern which may pass undetected.
  The work involved in discovering the pattern may frustrate you.
  Or, it may flatter your ego because you have the ability or knowledge
  to identify whilst others fail.

1

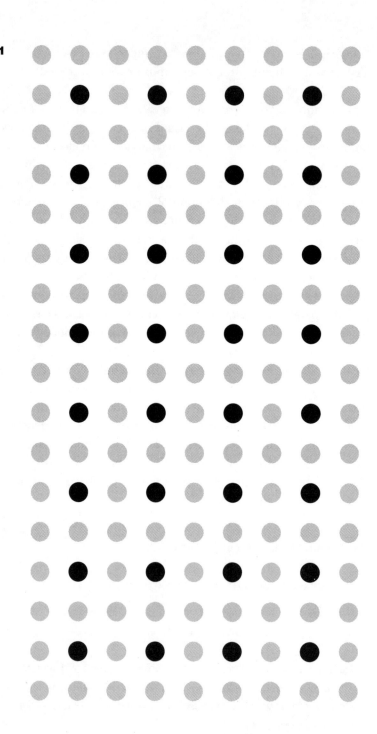

2

Test 8 • pattern failure

■ **Pattern 3**—a perceived error within a pattern becomes a focus of attention. The pattern becomes questionable or disappears altogether. Once spotted, such mistakes can become more recognised than the otherwise intended pattern.

Though it is possible that what you see represents part of a much larger whole, with the information on offer you cannot be certain.

Thought—a focal point is a powerful way to demand attention— whether deliberate or not.

Having set in motion a canvas of consistency, any abnormality, planned or otherwise, will promote itself. Through contrast it will stand out clearly. It will demand attention.

This is a double-edged sword: the error gets punished all the more, whilst the planned appearance of a deliberate highlight gains powerful prominence. Unfortunately, and all too commonly, it is the highlighted mistake which gains the most attention. All too often this is self-inflicted. These mistakes so commonly occur just because the consistency necessary for the identity to operate successfully is not sufficiently understood or acknowledged.

For many the issue of consistency is akin to boredom. 'Always the same' proves frustrating for those who tire of repetition—which on occasion may include most of us, especially when we lose the thread of the reasons and objectives of the identity. There is a need to beware of action or change prompted simply by restlessness or tedium. Remain alert to the waning concentration of the marketing department floundering through an unfocused desire for stimulation, when the real stimulus should be the ultimate goal of the overall identity.

3

■ **Pattern 4**—as is evident from Pattern 3, those who underestimate the importance of consistency when displaying their logo, or other elements of their identity, deliver these errors directly to their target audience.

Imagine 'Logo 1' is the logo of a company as displayed throughout its premises, advertising and literature.

At first glance, the logo may appear generally consistent. It certainly reads the same. Yet only five of these logos are strictly identical. Some inconsistencies are more obvious than others. You should take time to note your degree of blindness to these.

Be careful, because what you currently see as an acceptable level of consistency may not be consistency at all.

Once inconsistencies become apparent to an audience, they will inevitably be seen to represent a lack of systematic management or procedure. They must decide whether this inconsistency is deliberate or accidental. If the logo is inconsistent, then why should the integrity of that company's products prove to be any different? And, though you have not yet been introduced to them, what expectations do you have about this company's sales force? 'Erratic' springs to mind.

All this through the sole presentation of the logo, the tip of a much greater whole identity. Beyond the presentation of the logo itself consistency should be implemented at all levels of your communication, however insignificant some may at first appear. Your zeal for achieving not only consistency of appearance, but ever-increasing standards of the same in all your identity says and does will repay you in producing an identity of immense improvement and strength. Strong because all muscles pull in the same direction. Consistent because you do what you say you will do. You appear predictably predictable as a matter of standard expectation. Your consistency appears remarkable because competitors with less determination cannot match your continuity or regularity.

[4] **Logo 1**   **Logo1**   **Logo 1**

LoGo 1   **logo1**   **LOGO 1**

Logo 1   Logo 1   Logo 1

Logo 1   **L o g o 1**   **Logo 1**

LOGO 1   LOGO•1   **Logo 1**

Logo 1   **Logo 1**   **Logo 1**

Logo 1   **Logo 1**   **Logo 1**

You can take this to whatever extremes you desire. Let us consider just the regular size and positioning of a logo.

■ **Pattern 5**—unlike Pattern 4, these logos are consistent and therefore present a united appearance. Notice now how the whole becomes greater than the sum of parts—that consistency compounds.

Comparing Pattern 4 with Pattern 5, which company (Logo 1 or Logo 2) gives you the greatest confidence?

You may also ask yourself which of the two promises to keep its word. Now realise how much can be achieved through such an easy application of effort. What the organisation of 'Logo 2' offers in services or other content has not been discussed. We do not know what they do or how well they do it. Yet we can easily differentiate between this organisation's logo and Logo 1 in Pattern 4. There is a difference only quantifiable because of a thin veil of consistency which, despite no other information being available, speaks volumes. In such ways consistency leads an audience's opinions and expectations.

To summarise: to be consistent is to be predictable is to be measurable. Another word is 'quantifiable'.

To ram the point home again: tenacity to be consistent sets the strength of your identity. The greater your perception of consistency and desire to be consistent, the more strength your identity accrues. If you only pay this issue lip service, you will accordingly limit the strength of your identity. And it is a certainty that whatever level of consistency you have already achieved, there is a higher level to which you should aspire.

However high the actual quality of your product or service is, the consistency of your presentation controls how others may be willing to perceive you. A competitor with lower-grade products or services, who achieves a significantly higher standard of consistency, creates an advantage over you.

5   **Logo 2**   **Logo 2**   **Logo 2**

Logo 2   **Logo 2**   **Logo 2**

Logo 2   **Logo 2**   **Logo 2**

Logo 2   **Logo 2**   **Logo 2**

Logo 2   **Logo 2**   **Logo 2**

Logo 2   **Logo 2**   **Logo 2**

Logo 2   **Logo 2**   **Logo 2**

So here is your excuse to be a perfectionist and dictate your will throughout your organisation. Become obsessed—it's OK. To some, consistency may be seen as an uninteresting issue of little value—it may even seem counter to the instincts of many—but lack of it is corrosive to your identity.

Sadly, most people fail to understand the meaning of consistency. Even if you are nodding your head in agreement with what I have said so far, the chances are you still do not appreciate the commitment required or the degree of visual consistency necessary if your identity is to truly appear regular, disciplined and co-ordinated. Imagine you have a company which already enjoys some success and that your logo is cherished and much used. You believe it is used consistently, but look again. Take measurements, gather samples, cut them out, copy, stick them on a wall—look. Is what you see before you exactly the same? The same colour, spacing and proportion? Is the logo used consistently, are the supporting elements consistent, is it consistent in size and positioning? The levels of consistency go on. How seriously you challenge yourself and your organisation dictates the potency of your identity. This same potency can prove particularly invaluable when navigating through dramatic periods of change. Consistency pretends continuity and stability, whatever the changes it may be managing to conceal.

To ignore consistency and be consistently inconsistent labels you as an amateur. Very rarely can anyone behave like this and keep their integrity intact. The exception might be a performing artist or magician whose very act relies upon creating surprise and therefore unpredictability. Doing this consistently may be a crucial element to their identity and, with skilful management, may ensure it becomes an integral part of their success. However, your inconsistency may be less tolerated.

There are three types of consistency to concentrate on. As stated at the beginning of this chapter, you must ask yourself whether the mass of your identity belongs to you, your direct competition or perceived market area.

Consistency within market area

Market areas vary between old and established; young and rebellious; new and striving towards becoming established; or categories yet to be invented or acknowledged. In which market area do you choose to reside? You must decide this position.

You must also choose your level of conformity with that market and the competition within it. Is it comforting to your intended audience to be readily identifiable as belonging to a specific sector? If so, what is the identity of this sector? How far should you blend into or stand out from it? Decide your position—and your conformity with the positioning of others—before chance takes over.

If your market area has yet to be defined, who is defining it? Is it the media, your competitors, certain key personalities, or you? Set this market area firmly in mind. Invent your own if needs must. To a large extent all market areas are fictitious areas of common agreement. They exist because people agree upon their existence. Fit your identity within the boundaries you choose. Be deliberate.

Consistency within an organisation

This is the level of consistency within your organisation as understood and communicated by your marketing literature, exhibitions, press releases, signage, shop interior, vehicle livery, uniform and all other communication and display items. In fact, and of course, in everything you do. It is how you manage and regulate everyone within the team—and how you succeed or fail in the process.

In retailing it is irrelevant whether your shop is part of a larger retail chain or a unique outlet with a character of its own. The exterior and interior, stock, presentation and staff should form the shop's own consistency—however individualistic. Your consistency should be deep enough to sincerely match the qualities and values the identity intends to communicate. If not, you are a fake.

Individuality

An army intending to be seen and identified as a working unit needs to be dressed in the same uniform. If nothing else, it helps to know who to avoid shooting at. Unless you don't care: there is no known uniform for a bandit to wear, though a black hat is usually good enough in a Western. A covert force may avoid any form of dress code. Not seeking any visual identity, it literally wants to blend with the market.

But assuming you are a normal member of society, your dress or uniform, as everything else, should be relevant to the identity you wish to project. You have a need to be recognised today as well as tomorrow, next week or next year. A salesperson usually doesn't wear jeans one day, a suit the next, a miniskirt or shorts and a pair of flip-flops every alternate Wednesday and Friday, because confusion of this sort is not useful to his or her recognition or identity. Nevertheless, extremes of inconsistency eventually become consistency: you change uniform every single day because you are an unpredictable creative volcano—or clown—and that is just what you want your audience to believe.

The quest for consistency should never dominate an individual to the point where all individuality ceases, unless your aim is the forced regime of the combat unit or prison camp. In these circumstances the reasons may seem clear and justifiable for the objectives being set. However, the natural law is that people have a need to retain their individuality. This need should be taken into account or else you will surely offend them.

Inside the organisation, for example, you may want all your staff to wear the same red-coloured paper hats in every restaurant you own. You may have decided that it will form an effective part of your new identity, but how will your staff react? It may depend on how much they believe you are removing their individuality, and the validity or commonly shared benefits of doing so. The suppression of individuality in the interests of greater internal consistency must be treated with diplomacy and care, morale being such a delicate issue of trust and belief. From where else can staff gain their trust but recognition of and agreement with the consistency and values of their leaders?

If you are identified as a member of a group, you assume the values or perceived values of that group. If you judge those values to be worthy, you may be more willing to blend your identity with the greater whole. Otherwise, you resist. Witness children arriving at school in the morning and the differing manner in which they comply with a compulsory dress code. Their attitudes vary from total compliance to partial, individual interpretation or even refusal. Is this refusal the fault of the individual or the school?

Outside, beyond the confines of the organisation, you should not offend the individualism of your suppliers or customers either. Be aware of these boundaries and the actions you take when crossing them. In other words, don't take liberties with the identity of others unless you are prepared to pay the price. There are often situations in business when one identity must become a temporary partner or custodian of another. Often identities have need to support or endorse another. If your organisation is in communications or broadcasting you may well need to present the identities of others as part of your news bulletins or services. These identities may in turn have need to quote, endorse or promote you. Regardless, the issue of manners and attention to detail is often more important than some assume. If you respect the identities of others they are more likely to return the same consideration.

Personal consistency is not just uniform appearance. It can also be noticed in non-visual signals such as general attentiveness, willingness, manners, speech, writing, time-keeping and other forms of behaviour.

As with all the forms of consistency, the level and endurance people attain creates the combining force that binds together the critical mass and pattern we choose. Your consistency positions you within your marketplace. The pattern can set you apart and plays a major role in the amount of trust people both inside and outside the organisation are willing to offer you. You determine who will recognise and trust this pattern of consistency by its level of sophistication. Whatever the complexity of the pattern, you can and should determine the standard of this consistency and remain vigilant of any deviation.

Thought—the stronger the glue of consistency, the greater the underlying strength of your identity.

Culture

No escape

Thought—you cannot escape yourself.

You have culture. Not necessarily one of appeal or relevance to the tastes of your audience, though you may hope so, but the culmination of your evolution. To a large extent, regardless of how you present yourself, this culture will remain visible, a display of self, for better or worse, which cannot easily be disguised or ignored. To date, it comprises your journey of finding, advancement and failure. It is the history of your quest to fulfil the potential you believe is both necessary and possible.

Our perception of an organisation's, region's or nation's culture affects and effects us all. It can only be our 'perception' because these forms of culture, regardless of our experiences, cannot easily be defined by any set of laws, but rather are a series of seemingly commonplace agreements—commonalities noticeable enough to offer themselves for classification and agreement in the eyes of the onlookers.

These generalisations may be considered inaccurate and at variance with the viewpoints between the observer and the observed. Seldom will either share or agree about the same experience. What you may understand to be the national traits of your neighbour may be seen by them to be inexplicable, irrelevant or untrue.

In this manner, culture selectively judges, borrows, steals and recycles the combined experiences of all people and other cultures it encounters. It is built upon statement and reflection. Individuals and their shared history create these statements by opportunity, choice and necessity. Reflection about the roots, causes, needs, influences, hope and faith of these statements produces reiteration and further statement. Each buttresses the other until, like any structure, it becomes both recognisable and self-supporting. By this means the parts enforce and strengthen the whole. It is a living entity—a constant reworking and expression which draws reference to itself like a gravitational field, regardless of adversity, indeed often because of it.

Culture is a form of pretence. It pretends to be itself, at times may even parody itself, yet cannot escape being labelled itself whatever its action. Culture follows like a ghost in the minds of those who wish to follow, whether through respect, love or malice. For the cult figure or item, their culture may substantially outlive them, forming something more significant and enduring than the original. The cult may not necessarily be faithful to this original, instead, perhaps, it flourishes despite it. The origin becomes embellished or reduced by association or convenience and can become an icon capable of being revered, despised or hijacked. Only one thing is certain: nothing is sealed or safe from the abuse of time and usage.

Your culture is everything you have done, are doing, and are promising to do. It is also the full gamut of association you reside within—not necessarily what you say but how you say it—not necessarily what you wear but how you wear it. And so it permeates you. Its recognition is enforced and maintained through and by all aspects of its visual and audible appearance, recorded by whatever means, regardless of age, taste or type of reputation. To be able to fully comprehend your culture or another's and describe it in any meaningful detail is difficult, if not impossible. Culture is capable of being elusive and unaccountable, yet potentially all-encompassing and powerful. In particular beware your native culture and the culture you self-create, for it can dominate the parliament of your mind without election. You may not even register who controls whom. Regardless, you will commonly be judged by it, justly or otherwise.

Your organisation's culture also contributes towards your personal reputation. You may easily remain unaware of its full extent or influence because it has a tendency to escape scrutiny or definition—at least by you. After all, how can you hope to see yourself from outside when you are inescapably trapped within? Likewise, you can only judge the culture of others from the starting-point of your own culture.

And this is the main reason why, so often, issues of culture prevent an organisation from successfully expanding its interests beyond its existing social, regional or national boundaries. To the unskilled it will not be obvious what form the cultural negotiation or invasion should take. Proceed with caution or it could be your undoing.

Thought—culture permanently fights, wins or loses against itself and others.

The confusion of new

When encountering an unfamiliar culture you will experience confusion and a degree of insecurity. You will be concerned where the boundaries lie, such as taste, manners and the law. And the need to find out will be urgent. In your own culture, familiarity and knowledge allows you the capability to skilfully cross boundaries in the knowledge you are doing so. Now, crossing unawares, it can be fraught with consequence and danger.

A culture entirely different to your own in language, customs and value systems creates the maximum anxiety. Bewilderment can be enjoyable of course: an entertainment or holiday destination may be chosen for the difference of experience it offers. Indeed, when appropriate, uncertainty and insecurity can represent excitement or novelty. But confusion can also lead to suspicion, fear or the threat of acute danger. Unable to speak the native language, you must work

Illustration 8

X!X? XABE! Welcome

gzüs xwyzz ISSSSS?

Halt! qwwoab snoeyy

Nine signs. All are nonsense except for two—a pleasantry and an urgent instruction. Notice how your recognition and confusion divide, your mind gravitating immediately towards the messages you do understand.

hard to understand even the commonplace. Regardless of the work, there is comfort, if not huge relief, in recognition. The relief may be akin to the thirsty finding an oasis in the desert. And it may be just as life-sustaining. Finding these comfort points verifies progress and current position. If someone can understand the road signs they may hopefully reach their destination—as well as avoiding the many potential accidents. See Illustration 8 above.

Meeting a new organisation is no different. There is a need to locate and recognise its signposts. The same applies to learning any new subject, product or service; understanding the jargon of an unfamiliar technology or industry; finding your way through an airport terminal; operating a ticket machine, or finding the information you require in an instruction manual. Each has its own culture, its own systems of reference and understanding, the boundaries and rules of which some may not be able to comprehend. The success of navigation depends upon how lucidly that organisation wants to, or is able to, communicate its message, values and identity—its culture—and how much it can reciprocally accommodate the culture, access and relationship of others.

Thought—your identity and its culture should always aim to educate your audience.

Shepherd them, select them, and guide them—silently managing this process, alienating only those you choose to. But whatever you do, try not admit to it.

Translation

Understanding an organisation's culture, like another person's identity, is a process of decoding. Its visual identity (corporate identity) tells you one set of messages, whilst its culture of behaviour affirms or denies this. The reception interior and the logo say one thing, the dress and mannerisms of the receptionist say another; its marketing literature promotes it as a competent business but its external and internal signage system indicates the reverse.

When a client or supplier arrives at your premises, how must they judge you? How easily will they have followed your directions; found the correct parking place; located the correct entrance; opened the door the right way; felt comfortable with the procedure for entering the building further and judged the greeting they receive? If you are expecting them to wait in a reception area, in what circumstances must they wait and, whilst they do so, what visual messages are you offering them with regard to your taste, manners and integrity? This is perhaps their first experience of your culture. Your organisation inflicts this upon them. They have no choice. They are led to follow your wishes. They will assume that you are just as aware of the quality of their experience as they now have no choice but to be. Deliberate or not, this is the 'truth' you present them with—your character, your culture. They must entertain this before they may even meet you or partake in the business transaction that you have otherwise perhaps so meticulously planned.

Thought—just how hard must your audience work in order to reach the judgement you want them to make about your organisation?

The labour required and its benefits require a decision, an inevitable decision. Your culture or the culture of your organisation appeals or it doesn't appeal; it may be easy or difficult; it may require no initial understanding or else significant preparation, training or knowledge. The energy, ability and inquisitiveness of your audience may vary. These are the barriers which culture can present and which either enhance or inhibit the effectiveness of your corporate identity. If your culture persistently confuses or contradicts itself, then the time needed for decoding it extends accordingly.

Thought—how soon does your audience 'get it'?

Does your culture confuse your audience to the point where they would rather make a glib judgement of your apparent value than enquire further and find the truth you intend them to find?

False judgement may be the judgement of convenience: you wore the audience's patience down. They gave up part way through the maze you set before them. The obstruction they grew frustrated with became seen as your truth.

Beware, for it is the involuntary signals and mannerisms that reveal this inner character. And your audience is watching. Their assumptions about you may be that your apparently natural or unplanned appearance and behaviour is not only more fascinating than the formal message or display you are offering them, but more likely to prove a reliable and accurate estimation of your true identity.

Culture forms a large part of your identity—the part you may not have questioned enough. It is easy to become robotic without knowing it. Waking up from your sleep in order to question yourself is a frightening process of fiddling with foundations; the foundations upon which you believe you stand, even though you may know little of their construction. A common attitude is to defend yourself

Illustration 9

e   c   l

exce l n

exce l n

excell nt

excellent

How soon do you leap to a conclusion before waiting to understand
the complete message?

without compromise, expecting others to adhere or succumb to your culture, whether this is the best course of action or not. But why should you want others to put up with your behaviour if this contradicts the corporate identity you elsewhere promote so carefully? Disregarding the issues raised by your culture can only be due to laziness, ignorance or fear. Only courage of leadership can examine, change and manage as necessary.

The identity you appear to carefully plan and present to your audience needs verification to be believed. Verification must occur if you are to be believed. You will be judged. If your unguarded messages differ markedly from your deliberate corporate identity and communications, some or all credibility will be lost. Into this equation jump issues of taste and prejudice, and ignorance about your culture will further muddle the judgemental process.

What you don't say speaks the loudest. Your involuntary signals are trusted as genuine. The spontaneous, the improvised are believed. But what the audience cannot appreciate is the depth of detail and preparation within your presentation. The less you leave to chance, the more effortless your apparent improvisation and natural talent seem to be, providing the preparation remains as invisible as possible. Alternatively, pedantry advertised to the point of tedium can also prove to be a benefit. For example, an engineer who proudly claims to leave nothing to chance won't dazzle you with personality, but otherwise knowingly communicates thoroughness.

Thought—are you acting and, if so, how good are you? Where does the act end and reality begin?

Despite the utmost preparation, identity should never be just an act, a lifeless mantra with no spark of life. True, presentation sometimes requires forms of acting. The act should be intended to match the truth and the truth the act. Genuine is a powerful force and prerequisite for lasting, worthwhile identity. Frauds pretend identity but cannot own the values of the identity they attempt to copy, however convincing the copy may at first appear.

Illustration 10

QU**A**LI**T**Y REPAIRS

OPEN FOR BUSINESS

Involuntary signals speak the loudest.

Do not be surprised that the needs of presentation and acting can indirectly alter existing culture, behaviour and attitudes. Indeed they will, if the identity is doing its job of leadership—directing both organisation and its audience.

Self-awareness

How deeply you are concerned about the depth of your identity determines how life-changing your identity will become. Intelligent management recognises it as a vehicle for meaningful change and advancement. Identity can be the precursor and justification for excellence. Effective identity produces energy, motivation and move-ment—reorganisation, savings and reward. Identity should be the best investment you have ever made; if it proves otherwise, some-thing is seriously wrong.

Thought—your behaviour should remain relevant to the values of your identity.

Therefore how you behave, dress and talk should support and give credibility to each other. Audiences will have conscious and uncon-scious expectations. Relationships start and continue in the chase to affirm or deny these expectations. There is a speculation of give and take—the expenditure of patience, information and resources which may vary (often recklessly) depending upon the preferences of both you and your audience for protection or risk.

We all tend to form expectations about those we encounter, whether assessing by appearances alone or other more complete information, and these expectations demand to be affirmed or denied as quickly as possible. Judgement can be made by comparing the information you receive with what someone promises and, finally, what they deliver in relation to your values, often against a background of the opinions and rumours of others. Unless completely uninterested, you will seek confirmation as rapidly as possible. You seek to classify and file away your initial impressions. Indeed, you will want to believe these impressions whether they subsequently prove to be false or not. Simultaneously, they may be assessing you.

When we encounter someone or something new it is a process of exchange. What you offer and receive is an interactive process governed by many factors including need, reward and charity. It is a rapidly formed relationship forged by negotiation, yet often started by just a casual exchange. Its conclusion is often determined by the simple values of positive, negative or neutral: does the encounter leave you better or worse than if there were no encounter at all? In the future, will you tend to return, tolerate or avoid?

If you are the communicator, it is beneficial to be familiar with the culture of those you wish to communicate to, whether geographical, social or technical culture.

Like your audience, your own culture grew up around your feet because of your environment, circumstances, guidance and inherent character, or else was assimilated from others, perhaps without question, during a formative period of your development. Other culture may have been adopted through insecurity or fear—the culture of those you once considered to be competition, threat, idol or peer group. So you walked their walk, talked their talk. Perhaps you should ask yourself whether you still do.

Thought—if you assume the culture of others, and this to some extent is unavoidable, you also assume, in the eyes of those who view you, the same perceived values.

The culture of mass, for example a national, organisational, artistic or political movement's, labels you to your fair or unfair advantage or disadvantage. In other words it is a bridge or wall, depending upon the prejudices of your audience. In this way your reputation precedes you. What follows is something else. Bad reputations are as persistent as good reputations. Good or bad, the earlier they start, the deeper their roots.

Being aware of your culture transforms it into a resource. One which forever expands and from which you can draw: a collection of graphic devices and statements that can complement and promote your overall identity. This referral to yourself utilises the depth of your past as a reference point for all you do, confirming and enlivening the values and objectives of your entire identity.

Culture cannot by itself represent a complete identity. Although, for some, culture of location, product or service may be more communicative than any other form of graphic identity, it may simply begin and end there, especially if what you are offering is essentially an experience, location, or combination of the two: for example the idiosyncratic or exclusive restaurant where a carefully layered, eclectic weave of novelty, theme, delight and unique diversion creates a hypnotic and elusive atmosphere more interesting and communicative than any more obviously planned items (such as the graphics of logo or menu style) can achieve. In other words, what appears to be naturally good or interesting taste and uncontrolled identity is nothing of the sort. It is the most cunning identity of all—culture promoted as excellence.

Culture, natural or pretending to be, should enhance and add value to your identity. For example, interiors and costumes should further promote the values of your identity. They should never be considered irrelevant, because this display of culture supports the humanistic side of an identity where personality or personnel meet an audience. Where audience security is paramount, as for flight staff, police or security personnel, culture of environment, dress and conduct become elements especially vital to effective communication.

Thought—do you seek to dominate your audience, interact or disappear amongst them?

Illustration 11

middle ground

Who dominates whom—your identity or the identity of your audience?
If you meet halfway, what is to be judged the halfway point?

Walls and bridges

An organisation operating in culture or country other than its own can defy, blend or lose itself into the culture it is seeking to communicate to or work within.

If you are seeking to dominate the audience, are you expecting them to remain passive? For example, is little required of them? Or it is a process of meritocracy, where only those able or willing to understand will reach you? What level of interaction are you offering?

If you get it wrong, you may still be lucky. Honest miscommunic-
ation of culture may be forgiven because genuine speaks all languages and may be more emotionally powerful than either right or
wrong. Sincere and insincere are also common denominators. Some
things are more cross-cultural than others; for example, if greeted
by a radiant smile, providing a smile suits your expectations, you
may feel immediately at ease. Humour may also translate, but can
also prove unpredictable. Certain words, colours and symbols will
communicate regardless of language, whilst others may fail to bring
the recognition you intend. Culture to culture requires a translation
of knowledge, customs and manners as well as the languages used.
Common denominators that work regardless of language or any
other cultural differences are limited both in quantity and quality of
communication. Many can be clumsy or appear crass unless used
with care. Mankind may appear to be the same worldwide but culture dictates otherwise. The differences are not always visible. An
estate agent, when asked what single most important factor sells a
property, may be expected to use the cliché 'location, location—and
location'. Well, location has a lot in common with culture too. And
as for estate agents, some countries have no use for them, indeed
may never have heard of them. It is possible they never will.

A meeting of different cultures is the meeting of identities. To what
extent one acknowledges, challenges or modifies another is unpredictable. Invasion may seem a strong word, but one inevitably
invades the other on each and every level of confrontation. A meeting or exchange of influence can be an entirely balanced affair, or
more to the benefit of one than the other. You may be proud of your
culture, so may be your audience. You wish to defend your identity;
again, so may your audience. Proceed with caution!

Thought—in the meeting of cultures, how far do you expect to lead
your audience? How far are you prepared to allow them to lead you?

Your audience may positively wish to lose awareness of their own
culture in your presence. A cinema audience may wish this if convinced of the benefits of surrender—total absorption in the

entertainment, which they expect to gain pleasure from. Alternatively, a business or political audience may react to this as being unacceptable, aggressive or even warlike. If total loss of culture or identity is the only option available to an audience, they may consider their corresponding reaction can only be total compliance or refusal. What choices are you giving them? This manner of interaction you place before them determines the workings of your relationship. The balance of this interaction should be planned. What you may receive is likely to match what you may give. Of course, the nature of the product or service, to a large extent, dictates the necessity to make concessions to the culture of others. What you offer may be unique enough to be considered cross-cultural, or render the differences between cultures irrelevant, inconsequential or even trivial. Some subjects justify more dominance than others, and not just the dominance of markets and audiences but the staff you employ, whom likewise you may be expecting submission from. What you seek and demand from others is part of the bargain you intend to strike. At one end of the spectrum it is market forces, whilst at the other the detail of manners. If you are judged to be rude when intending to be polite, you had better research the rules within which you are expected to operate.

Thought—power becomes culture and culture becomes power.
Use it wisely.

Character

Interaction

Just as we are able to perceive the personality of the individual, the character of an organisation or product is very real. You encounter an identity; a product; a corporate communication; the building of an organisation—all exude personality.

Character is perceived through the experience of our senses. As we hear, touch, taste, see and smell we estimate and formulate our opinion through one or more of these doors of perception. The greater the number of senses engaged, the more influential the experience. Each sense furnishes the recipient's mind with all manner of verifiable or implied information. For example, you can hear whether someone is loud, but you can also 'see' loudness by the implication of other signals such as vibrant colour or forceful action. Arguably, the strongest sense is what we see, and, as argued at the beginning of this book, we all tend to believe what we see. This general truth can now be developed for, to a lesser or greater extent, we also believe what we hear, touch, taste or smell. Such limitations make us human.

So an identity can appear loud or retiring, passive or assertive. It can create the impression of youthfulness, maturity, antiquity, impertinence, humour, seriousness, calmness, an activity or energy level of any sort, or any other combination of characteristics you choose to communicate by design, or hit upon by accident.

These issues are issues of interaction. They are about how your identity connects to or involves the audience.

Thought—how much does your identity involve your audience beyond what is necessary to the function of the service or product being identified?

For example, a vehicle is a mode of transport. It gets you from A to B. Sports cars are also a means of transport, but one which seeks to involve the user beyond the elemental function of the former. It can accentuate this engagement to various levels of passion, for some even ecstasy. The addition of a flamboyant or outrageous colour, shape, noise or other aspect of design can be defended as being within the realms of personality, the difference it is intending to project. In extreme cases, such as the rare, exotic or classic car, the product may even go so far as to involve the user in its intrinsic fragility or unreliability, provided the user is forgiving or indulgent enough to appreciate this excess of personality. Here the very personality of the characterful product becomes both its excuse and defence against those who would criticise it on the grounds of reason only, for the exercise of reason alone cancels anything beyond itself. In other words, passion or romance is one of life's more irrational actions, and it is this element of needing or expecting more than just the rational which we seek to justify in so many of our choices and purchases. Call it thrill, excitement, passion, romance or exuberance, the irrationality of passion exerts a powerful influence over us all.

Where the application of passion is appropriate it may work wonders, glossing over otherwise unforgivable features or consequences. Elsewhere it renders the organisation or product inappropriate, unacceptable or distasteful.

Classic or romantic?

Marketing an organisation or product with too much perceived design hype is a mistake when its exclusivity or desirability demands that it be sought after or requested rather than 'sold', prostituted, offered or promoted too freely. This is about judging both the dignity and distance you wish to set between your organisation and the tastes of your audience. Other factors of design also greatly affect the presentation of your identity, such as colour, shape, size and space issues—all of which set its tone.

Consider that the graphics you choose for a logo design fall into one of two categories: classic or romantic.

Classic graphics are those defendable by straightforward reason. They may literally represent you, your location, marketplace, product or service. They don't contain any real surprise or major pretence. They do not seek to divert or deceive the audience away from the true or literal nature of the product. At most, they provide a low level of shock to an audience and do not overtly challenge them or their expectations. This is the recipe for being traditional (which can also be interpreted as old-fashioned), placing you at a predetermined distance behind current fashion, time or mode. Alternatively, to position yourself slightly behind the leading edge of fashion usually translates as smart—for the time being—until fashion moves, as it inevitably does. Frequent review of identity can help control this, just as some confectionery products, despite their market launch several decades ago, adjust their appearance without too noticeably appearing to change.

If classic graphics are fairly easily assimilated, romantic graphics break with the expected. They contain a shock value which promotes a concept of newness, the unexpected, the new philosophy, theory or practice, and, of course, the controversial. These graphics build an element of risk into an identity and present you with a problem, for they will test you and your power or weakness of logic, whether it is your identity or another's that you are viewing. These graphics are abstract—often a metaphor—that can vary from almost meaningless to double or multiple meaning in order to promote their concept. They attempt to invade the audience as a suggestion to break a previous mould. They work through a connection which disrupts expectations; an exploitation or coincidental connection between two formally unconnected thoughts that compels or appears to form a new truth; a missing link which communicates its previous absence as an idea, story or emotion; a transformation, journey or movement; an escape or apparent removal of imaginary boundaries; or, in general, an emphasised or exaggerated plea and use of fantasy which creates an identity beyond the truth of the individual, product or organisation's reality.

Your willingness to change, alter or reinvent reality, and use a level of fantasy which you feel beneficial, acceptable and sustainable for the time necessary to serve your objectives, should be carefully discussed and decided upon as part of your brief to yourself and your designer.

Presenting an identity that attempts to transform or lead an audience in a direction other than they previously intended is a surprise; and surprise produces reaction, which if carefully thought through and implemented, can produce spectacular and positive results. But surprise can excite in both directions—a polarisation that can just as easily stun your audience into inaction as action, define taste or create distaste, liberate or threaten insecurity, create or destroy prejudice, validate or outlaw, attract or repel. It hardly needs to be stated that accurately predicting the impact of your intended surprise is important.

Thought—excessive use of fantasy—in logo, graphics or names—can weaken your credibility.

Such excess will tend to limit the potential size of your audience. Your plans may be to defy current beliefs and usher in a new era of technology or other advancement, but how much of the identity you are communicating constitutes the truth, whatever the position and climate of current opinion?

The suitability, appeal, cleverness and humour that a logo or logo-type suggests must be appealing enough to succeed when first encountered, yet endure and hopefully extend its appeal over several years.

Thought—a design can be too appealing on first sight.

A design should not necessarily satisfy your appetite and reveal its entire content too soon. The most successful designs radiate their energy and engage you over a longer timespan. Their initial impact may be deliberately ordered, and often simplified, in order to ensure the desired longevity. The old adage of 'less is more' is so often proved true. A designer presenting a simple idea should be given the grace and time to allow the design to work upon you.

Don't be guided solely by your preliminary reactions to the presentation of the idea—for if presented to you by a designer, be aware that this is an introduction untypical if not impossible for your eventual audience. They will not and cannot share the same experience as you. Your approach, relationship with your designer, responsibility and attitudes towards risk and fear cannot be theirs. Instead, however favourably or otherwise you feel about the presentation, I recommend you spend a minimum honeymoon period of three days to fall in or out of love with any significant design or creative proposal. Build time into your schedules to accommodate such periods.

Age

Age is also a major feature of an identity. This is not just the age of the organisation or product, but all signals of age from the period of the premises, fashion and technology you employ to the psychological aspects of age, such as signals of attitude and morals.

Often a combination of ages will need to coexist within your identity. For example, a young organisation for which youthfulness is a positive attribute deserving to be promoted may also 'use' elements of establishment or history, such as antique furniture or old technology, and perhaps mix them with leading-edge artefacts and

furnishings or practices. But they can only successfully and intel-
ligibly achieve this if they keep to their firmwords. In other words,
be as eclectic as you wish, regardless of age, providing the common
denominators between these objects or characteristics bind all
together at that very point where your identity fully energises and
excels: your firmwords.

Gender

It is worthwhile asking yourself how masculine or feminine your
identity appears to be through its presentation and content. The
answer may depend upon the character of the organisation or
product being promoted as well as audience preference. Notions of
sexual orientation, including the option of sexual neutrality, are
both noticeable and manageable through visible features such as
shape and colour as well as attitudes and mannerisms.

An identity becomes categorised by the culture of the audience it
exists to persuade. This audience will gauge the physical appearance
and interaction of the identity against the yardstick of their culture.
For example, depending upon the politics of taste and attitude, the
application of certain colours will be suggestive of gender, however
pronounced or subliminal these suggestions may be. Likewise, the
weight and shape of typefaces and other decorative graphical elements hold potential connotations of sexuality.

When these factors are combined, whether consciously or unconsciously, they become most persuasive. These signals effect all five
senses, including smell, which, although perhaps the least likely of
them all to influence an identity, is for some organisations, such as
those in the cosmetics industry and some retailers, a valuable and
undeniable component: for example, where ambience or atmosphere are influential to those who enter a retail area. Like muzak,
smell is not always consciously noticed. When it is, we tend to form
an opinion. Why else do we become compelled to categorise the
scent of perfumes into notions of his or hers, or else consciously promote them as being cross-sexual? Pour femme or homme colour too,

such as the issue of pink or powder blue or the neutral alternative or primrose yellow for the newborn baby's nursery (or the deliberate avoidance of all three), will exercise the minds of many a parental home decorator. But it also exerts a wider influence, such as the choice of décor for a passenger terminal, the exterior and interior colour schemes for a range of automobiles, the predominant colour on a brochure or uniform. Be aware that there will be many crucial or sensitive colour decisions where merely choosing the wrong colour may wreak havoc upon the desired identity simply because of a contradiction or confusion you have unwittingly presented to your audience. In addition, even if you do not share the superstitions or traditions of your audience, you should make sure that you are aware of the gender boundaries you may be crossing. Ignore them at your peril.

Deliberate gender-crossing, for example a logotype or other graphic with a heavy typeface of masculine appearance—such as an ultra bold or Egyptian slab serif font—for a predominantly female product, where a degree of finery or sensitivity would normally have been expected, can be effective if you can be certain of controlling the controversy that this kind of cross-dressing can cause. Through stark contrast, in this example presented in a defiance of common custom or expectations, you may have created a powerful and overt statement of daring. Alternatively, you may be disastrously off the mark. The subject matter often dictates beyond negotiation this balance of gender.

Upon first analysis, an earthmoving machine hardly seems to be a feminine product. But imagine that this particular contractor is owned and operated by female personnel within a nation or culture where this would still be considered to be unusual. If so, the marketing department may realise that this disruption of expectations (and the controversy it therefore produces) provides useful publicity and is therefore a positive addition to the identity.

In summary, considerations of gender can be finely argued down to the smallest of details. Often an identity must exist as a mixture of differing gender signals in order to reflect both its staff and audience's preferences alike. Even so, some areas of an organisation's business can benefit or suffer through its deliberate or indiscreet application. This is regardless of any existing legislation relating to sexual equality.

Names

Call me what you like

At the centre of your identity is your name. Self-explanatory or abstract in its communication, it is the pivot around which all other elements must attach themselves. Name assists definition of character, suggesting clues of age, gender, nationality and other attributes of personality.

Thought—you offer your audience two items: your appearance, however welcome, and your name, however noteworthy.

A name signals difference. It is a label definable by attitude; a threshold or entrance to that which it represents; direction; past, current or future position; departure or turning; a label of promise or foreboding depending upon audience point of view, whatever the qualities of its signal.

Something, anything, exists because of its label. It need not physically exist: it can just as easily be rooted in the fantasy or abstract imagination of the mind as any other form of reality.

As a label it asks for verification, recognition or other response. You recognise the signal of the label, want to, or remain ignorant. You may require a reason or other stimulus in order to inspect closer. A major or minor alert, a name indicates there is more than may immediately meet the eye. It offers definition without necessarily hurrying to explode the underlying nature of the substance it presents or conceals. This label may be the first formal or informal notification of what you are about to encounter, and so is an invitation for judgement, though often in combination with other information, appearance or manner. A name endorses—in haze or pin-sharp focus—by association, deed or other information, however scant or available. The role of graphic design is to positively manage this information, which, in turn, helps to lead to these judgements.

If you have no name, you will need to invent one. There may be urgent pressure to decide, as you cannot trade legally without one. The process of searching for and agreeing upon a name can become either a flippant affair or else the beginning of an agonising period of research and contention. Commonly, a name is adopted hastily, with scant regard to how appropriate it may be, not just during the short term but in the distant future. The implications, which may arise through repetitive usage or the unexpected interpretations and constructions of others, also need to be carefully scrutinised.

Construction and maintenance of content must involve more than name alone. A name can seldom carry the weight of an identity by itself, or at least not unaided for any long duration of time. It is merely the label, which represents the greater whole—the pleasing compère or master of ceremonies whose task is to introduce and appear to manage the show. All aspects of an organisation's operations must work in unison behind the name(s) it employs or chooses to promote, supporting the whole in order to achieve the necessary depth and unison of purpose required so as to remain effective. If you have no sensible choice but to work with an existing name, still ask all the same questions.

If a name is a combination of one or more names, question the seniority between one and another. Are all names equal or some more equal than others? Is the new upstart more valuable than the old master, or vice versa? Check which name is subservient to another. Does one name endorse another? Are any of the words interchangeable as part of a larger identity, for example a product or place name that changes to suit the occasion? Are there any names, or parts of names, likely to be changed or phased out at any point in the future? In this manner consider the components and other issues within the name.

Many expect to achieve notoriety, uniqueness or originality through invention of name alone. The name you choose may be dynamite—good or bad depending on which side of the explosion you stand. Meanwhile, many an otherwise ideal choice of name is eliminated without enough consideration simply because at this early stage—perhaps as a scribble on a notepad—it appears too nondescript.

The larger the geographical area you intend the name to operate within, the more valuable the name which can successfully cross national or cultural boundaries without the interpretation of language. These boundaries can be from one social group to another, market to market or country to country. Certain words, characters or numbers are more widely acceptable than others. A name which excels itself in one area of operation may be commercial suicide elsewhere. Examine the issues of culture in order to decide how best to penetrate each market to the benefit of the whole operation.

Further mileage is gained when a name also actively contributes towards your objectives through its literal or suggestive use of language, its genuine power of reputation (self-earned or through association with another's reputation) or authority of endorsement. Combined with graphics, hopefully, its potential to be memorised in the eyes and ears of your audience is significantly boosted. This certainly includes censoring within the promoted name any unnecessary legalese or words of dubious or defunct value which add little or nothing to the cause.

The durability of a name needs to match that expected of the identity. It needs to work long term on a slow fuse because, for most, long-lived reputation and appeal is ultimately more beneficial and profitable than just initial infatuation. Of course the ideal is to successfully manage both ends of this scale: be powerfully attractive upon first impression and remain so indefinitely.

The tonality with which a name is spoken and the rhythm with which it can be read also sets a certain ambience and expectation. These assumptions are connected with associations in the mind of the viewer derived from their personal experience, taste, culture or any other former information, rumour or suspicion. Connotations of character and quality, together with the uniqueness of a name, pitch it into our awareness. Like driftwood on a beach it stays there until swept further or carried away by successive waves.

Thought—impediments of a name become obvious when communicating verbally.

All names need verbal management because the clarity and phonetics of the names you employ are significant to success.

Listen to the manner in which you or your team instinctively answer the telephone. Do the names you use need to be spelt aloud in order to clearly or efficiently communicate or enforce? Perhaps the phonetics give rise to certain irritations when used verbally? How often do you find yourself needing to correct an enquirer, in order to prevent confusion? These are alarm bells you should take serious note of. You may be able to counter some of these problems by a change of pronunciation, punctuation or spelling. If not, you should consider changing the name.

Memory of name can be aided to an astonishing degree by visual appearances. Visual presentation is guaranteed to transform any name, often despite being poorly executed. With skilled typographical treatment or added graphics an otherwise unremarkable name can assume a new persona, no longer solely reliant upon the nature of its sound or basic letterform.

Thought—familiarity escapes proper interrogation.

Regardless of the effectiveness of the name you choose, or must use, its ability to make a first impression will, though repeated usage, wane. The shock of the new gradually erodes for all who must, through familiarity, become less sensitive to or mindful of the qualities of its first impression. As though climbing inside the name, assuming it, consuming it or being unwillingly subjected to it, the weary can longer judge with impartiality. For those past the issue of acceptance, first impressions of the name become demoted, or diluted to a newer level of confusion—a series of other more fundamental experiences, such as the organisation or product itself.

Meanwhile, those who yet remain to be attracted or convinced may, depending upon the nature of their introduction, only notice or begin to do so by the flag-waving of your name alone. Hence the strain to force into the invention of a new name far more import than it is fair to expect it to contain. Reputation needs to be earned. It must follow name—hopefully with the minimum of delay—but the name cannot contain reputation from zero hundred hours, launch day one: it must accrue. Only then may your reputation precede you.

Thought—a name is a starting-point of awareness. And awareness breeds reputation.

Even for an established 'name', reputation needs to be substantiated daily. A name in isolation is an empty vessel. It gathers weight of importance from the fraternity of the other elements it must mix with. A snowflake becomes a snowball becomes the snowman. And it can melt away just as easily through neglect or changes in environment, fashion or attitude. Names can be faddish, suddenly bursting into fashion, departing with a bang or whimper or reappearing from another age as though newly cleaned. Words, through usage, often beyond control, can significantly alter in inference, sometimes being involuntarily rendered unfit for their original purpose—on occasion overnight and without warning. There is a certain graveyard in the land of Identity with numerous unworkable names, wrecks of neglect and glorious failures of names. Time may revive some whilst permanently condemning others.

The problem with names

Thought—rule number one: don't trust them.

Never take any name or, for that matter, any descriptive word for granted. Challenge all the names used within your identity and communication materials by interrogating them for meaning, source and relevance.

Thought—names obstruct as much as they construct.

For example, if someone innocently asks you what it is you do for a living, how do you answer them? What terminology, qualifications or title do you print on your business card? Looking at your job title, where did this title originate? Your convention or that of another? Does it extend or limit your impact? Is it boastful or modest, explanatory or misleading? In short, is it helpful, or of no use at all? All words are suspect. What does a word mean in terms of your identity? What does it add? Who is it meant to impress—you or the client? Often in business it is best to say nothing. Speak when you need to and contemplate what you say, for so often the terminology of others is allowed to 'invade' an identity unchallenged. Beware, for it steals your thought patterns—words are often the building bricks of thought. Change the bricks and the building changes.

All names and terminology should be questioned in terms of what represents fashion, truth (as opposed to fantasy) and that which, where possible, conforms to your firmwords, therefore adding to your reputation and integrity.

And remember consistency. Once you have vetted the names you are to work with, use them consistently in speech and written material. Pay attention to word detail again and again—and again.

Do not over-use names but use them sparingly. Too many names to digest at once or over-usage of a name can upset the flow of the real message.

Thought—effective communication should lead to the names, not be obstructed by them.

Often the audience must struggle to understand what is being said. Boredom, fatigue and insult—do not inflict them on yourself, your team or your audience. Consider whether the terminology within your literature is helpful, accurate and understandable. Understand that a name or description can be viewed as being positive, negative or neutral in message. Is the polarity of your terminology therefore suitable to the messages you are attempting to communicate? And, is it also memorable?

Thought—an audience must be given the opportunity to remember your name. Then they must want to.

Think for a moment about the relationship between how well known your name is now, and how well known you would like it to become in the future. Then think about how memorable your name and the presentation of it is for the audience you hope will remember. Memorable names are valuable. Experiment with names in order to gain the maximum advantage from their presentation. But, long or short name, be cautious when reducing, especially if the result is a group of initials, which though possibly memorable may be more faceless than you imagine.

If the initials are obviously memorable, you are fortunate, for more usually they represent a dull and commonplace barrier which limits memory recall—although calm, steady and predictable (even if considered uninteresting) may be just the attributes to suit your objectives.

If you are expecting your audience to become familiar with the full names for which the initials stand, beware that you are not demanding too much or making unwise assumptions about the patience or interest of your audience. In addition, you need to evaluate the possibility that, should your organisation develop beyond the point where the original meaning of those initials becomes an irrelevance, impediment or embarrassment, you may be faced with either a change of name or else the abandonment of explanation—the origins are demoted to an anecdote of history. The abstract nature of the initials must now stand with only their remaining merits of distinction, character or memorability.

Initials that form an acronym can be extremely effective as long as they don't insult, irritate or in time become rendered counter-productive to your original aims. Over time, whether as a result of your activities or the progression of society and its language as a whole, acronyms can become assimilated into English and adopted as nouns. Yet the benefit of acronyms is that they can convey complex or lengthy messages which would otherwise be too unwieldy to communicate so easily, assuming they are communicated with style and credibility, anything else being the sign of an amateur.

If the name is a group of initials, how commonplace is the first initial? The importance of this becomes obvious when listed alphabetically in a directory. Some characters of the alphabet are more subscribed to than others. You may be surprised to find that even your complete group of initials is also used by another organisation, albeit perhaps in a different market area. The resultant hindrance of communication may be a major obstacle to your prime objectives: for example, if you are a national or global organisation expecting the general public to remember and recognise your initials, those initials had better be unique as well as being memorable, or else budget for a long-haul advertising and public awareness campaign.

But these points do not just apply to initials, for all names can be just as forgettable: witness most people's difficulties remembering the names of those introduced to them upon the first meeting.

In general, do not make things more difficult by including within your name any unnecessary words of dubious benefit. Each word should ideally earn its keep. After all, you already, or intend to, invest a good deal of your resources into promoting this name to your audience.

Brand

What is brand?

This book is not intended to be a substitute for a dictionary or indeed a history lesson, but some clarification and explanation of the word 'brand' will serve us well, if only because the word is so often bandied about with too little thought as to its true meaning or correct application.

Brand originally meant 'torch'. To fire an item fresh in the furnace was to brand. So a flaming torch, presumably wooden, certainly combustible, was a brand. Subsequently it became applicable to all things new. It was also customary to mark offending vagabonds with a red-hot iron either on the chest or left cheek. Until 1879 army deserters were also 'branded' below their left nipple (apparently the right one was safe) with either a D for Deserter or with BC for Bad Character. During this time a merchant's or excise mark on a commodity or article also became known as a 'brand'. Then cowboys arrived on our cinema screens and branding became the burnt mark of ownership on cattle hides and farmers' stock generally. The good guy finding and shooting the cattle rustlers somehow sticks in the cranium, and off the world goes talking about this brand or that brand or issues of branding, with no division between what identity means on the one hand and branding means on the other.

On one level it seems quite simple: brand is identity. Which means it can be a product or service identity, providing the item is clearly differentiated from any other similar product or service. A brand can be visually separate from the identity of the parent organisation, or alternatively the two can present themselves as being identical, in which case the organisation is brand, and brand is organisation.

So what purpose does the word 'brand' serve? The point is that, although in most respects a brand is just an identity—the two words casually appearing to be interchangeable—there is a subtle inference in a brand, which travels beyond that of a plain identity. All identities can pretend to be a brand, but there is a fine boundary between pretence and accomplishment.

True brands assume a power of their own. It is possible to wake up to find that what we thought of as merely an infant or unremarkable product identity has, in the eyes of others, become acknowledged as a brand. This occurs because it is perceived to be so in the eyes of the audience. They confer this status upon an identity, not the owner or creator of the identity. Via graphics, presentation and some acknowledgement of success, achievement or reputation, an identity enters this arena—a higher level of acceptance. It is, by audience vote, a promotion in rank for what was previously considered to be just an another identity, however clever its design and presentation. Through synergy and acceptance, this identity enacts more than the total sum of its parts. It represents more than before. The previous intangibles of the identity take on a new level of understanding or acceptance, and in doing so become tangible, or more so, perhaps now needing to be supported by the next layer of intangibles (in which case, re-examine the firmwords). The identity, now a brand, stands for something much deeper or clearly defined than ever before. Foolish any owner who mismanages this success, because they do not understand why their identity has transformed itself into a brand.

Of course most pretend brand before the award is given. They blindly hope, or else assume, it will be theirs, and they may succeed for as long as their advertising budget can fund the illusion. This is acceptable and profitable providing it remains plausible to those they are trying to convince. True brand status does not rely solely on a publicity machine, though its perpetuation and market penetration benefit from consistent promotion. Being seen is not the only entry test for the would-be brand, because many brands persist and thrive in the imaginations of the audience with minimal and, sometimes, no advertising. In this regard, a brand is a credibility test. It has an inherent energy to communicate itself and an audience will choose it through acceptance and recognition of this.

All other identities, which are yet to win this lucrative status, are purchased because of a less stable or unsubstantiated set of promises. They remain to be accepted with the same level of trust. They pretend their throne, and may do so with lavish pomp and ceremony. Meanwhile the true brand glides almost regally with a self-confidence the pretender cannot experience. It feeds off its own power, if it must, whilst the pretender constantly requires the stoking of fuel, or will peter out.

But the effects of brand, true or pretend, are ubiquitous. Whether by accident or choice, all products, including the most basic commodity, assume part of their value from the identity or brand of the seller. Difference is everywhere. It may be the consequence of being inherently unique, an invention rocking the world by its distinction. In addition, the difference can be accentuated or entirely manufactured by packaging and logo in order to guide its recognition and acceptance into the desired markets.

Contributors to brand

All aspects of identity contribute to the notion of brand. No product sold through a retail outlet or distributor can escape it. As an extreme example, let us consider the humble potato, which you may think needs little identification. In most Western countries potatoes are a commonplace commodity and are therefore known and trusted as an unpackaged product. Unpackaged also means the product can be handled and inspected for quality. For those whose business it is to know more, there are clearly identifiable varieties of potato, not packaged varieties, but seed varieties, named and known for their different characteristics, including cooking qualities. As this chapter explains, the act of naming is the first step in any form of identity; other forms of visual identification follow, such as age, size and colour.

Despite these technicalities (and why should it surprise us that all products, however basic they may appear to be, have such complexities?), a potato can be sold in a simple manner, unlabelled or not, for example by a market trader, where the only issue of brand seems to be appearance versus price; but not just the appearance of the potato, the appearance and manner of the display and vendor, too. Therefore the market trader's set of values and personality transfer to the identity of the potato on display, which may be exactly the identity of the potato you wish to purchase.

Alternatively, a large supermarket can provide a more complex context. It is indoors and therefore likely to be a cleaner, more clinical environment. The name of the supermarket may belong to a familiar chain or brand, which you may or may not acknowledge. However, it is probably either heated or air-conditioned, with an array of electric lighting, background music, in-store promotion, labelling and packaging to enhance both the display and convenience of purchase. Perhaps the supermarket also provides a choice of washed or fresh-from-the-soil potatoes, information on alternative varieties to choose from and a description of the cooking attributes of each variety. Self-service may appeal to you— the ability to select, without supervision, for yourself—and a less personal service may also suit your personality or mood. Again you are presented with appearance versus price. Again, the supermarket's set of values and personality transfers to the identity of the potato on display, which may be the potato that appeals to you. Your preference, as well as notion of convenience, is largely influenced by identity. And this a humble potato.

Not all products have qualities which can be judged by appearances alone. This also includes potatoes, for only when they are cut open can some crop diseases be seen. As another example, a second-hand machine may only display its external condition. The internals—its true specification and quality—may remain open to speculation. Its brand or packaging (the product, environment, identity and display of the dealer, should there be one) provide the only clues other than operating the machine and running a comprehensive test. Even then, its perceived quality and reliability may be an opinion created to a large extent by the previous success of its brand in your comprehension. A well-known name may be more highly valued than a lesser-known one, or the opposite may be true, because desire and reputation are not necessarily linked to mass awareness. Previous experience of these brands will influence your decision. But a well-known identity can also be a weak one. Perhaps it is considered insincere or inappropriate to the product or service being offered. At worst, it advertises itself as an identity to avoid because of its past reputation or perhaps simply because of the fear of the unknown through lack explanation or education. Perhaps it is to be avoided because of fashion—too fashionable or not fashionable enough. It may be refused because it confuses by sending contradictory signals which make the intangibles it pretends to promote conflict with the perceived reality of the product.

Thought—brand proposes to be a guarantee of quality.

Other manufacturers may remain anonymous, either by desire or accident. If by choice, perhaps it is an unscrupulous trader waiting to trap you with a sudden inconsistency, or a trader choosing not to stand by the reputation of the product. It could be a form of sublime understatement destined to appeal only to those with some other predetermined or exclusive knowledge. All this is for the market to decide—highly enlightened or deeply ignorant.

Let us return to the potato. On first impression it appears to be unbranded, yet the trader unavoidably endorses the potato with his or her own identity, an identity which they may either have planned or be blissfully unaware of. The point is that, for a vendor, the choice exists to identify any product in accordance with their aims. Unlabelled, therefore unidentified or branded, a product may realise only a fraction of its potential value, whilst the value of a brand, though it requires the full support and commitment of an identity, may easily exceed the value of the tangible assets of an entire company. The value of a brand can float like the share value of a quoted company. For this reason it can be referred to as 'brand equity'. Choose to manage this equity or risk it managing you.

Equity

For manufacturers, distributors and retailers, the equity of brand is worthy of extreme concentration. For all, the success or failure of a brand can rapidly transfer to profit or loss. This is more sensitively felt at the two 'sharp ends' of brand: manufacturing and retailing; but a distributor equally needs to watch the value of the stock they choose to carry. A more distant beneficiary or victim of brand is the service provider who rides upon the larger waves of the economy but who may also draw partial or total reliance from a particular brand or area of branded products. Fashion, new or potential legislation and sudden demand for products activate fluctuations in brand value and problems for those whose livings may directly or indirectly rely upon their success.

The more fashionably dependent the brand, the more volatile its tendency to shoot up or down in value. Therefore the decision to expand on the back of its success should be made with caution. The dedicated production line, warehouse extension, display area or expensive promotion may be the best or worst decision you are about to make.

Thought—a brand is an act of discrimination.

And as previously discussed, so are all names. Without branding, a 'face cream' is only a cream, indeed a cream of unknown quality. Only by the intention to identify or brand can the focusing word 'face' can be included. Other elements of the identity may then further develop and more finely tune this product to its intended market.

Thought—many products exist in the minds of the audience only because of brand.

Loyalty

Branding invites a purchaser to make easy choices. Markets tend to be increasingly complex and bewildering in the choice they offer consumers. Within this proliferation of brands and dramatic increase of apparent choice, each brand attempts to justify its own voice and personality. Each one is an attempt to speak clearly through the centre of this confusion—speak to those it chooses—communicating regardless of middlemen or any other arbitrator or negotiator standing between brand and its devotees. It attempts to speak beyond distributor or retailer, directly to the hearts and emotions of its audience. The stability that the truly successful brand brings to the manufacturer mirrors the stability it also brings to the retailer and distributor. It can become an intricate relationship where each calls upon the loyalties of the others, for what may otherwise be only a faceless or price-driven commodity becomes a recognised brand of acute need to manufacturer, retailer and customer alike.

Thought—a brand should engender affection and loyalty.

You may want to change the identity of a product or maybe cease its production, but will your audience allow it?

If successful, the child becomes more persuasive than the parent. Like a developing star performer the brand takes centre stage and captures the show. A good manager should manage from behind to protect the protégé's progress. Brands assume influence and power, after which wealth can quickly follow, only to be followed again by all those wishing to mimic, or unable to think beyond mimicking the original. This is an attempt to borrow or steal their show, should you allow it. Organisations need to protect their brands, which means being prepared to be dictatorial and aggressive where necessary. This is especially true when one also realises that the strong visual identity of any product also protects its invention. Patents expire, but the value of a brand can live on. Even when it is lawful for others to copy a patent, it probably isn't lawful for them to copy its visual identity. So if an organisation can ensure that its identity is synonymous with the invention, in the long term the identity will extend the profitability and market of the original patent.

Structure

The need for structure

A clearly defined structure for an identity is necessary if an audience are to be expected to understand an organisation and how it conducts its operations. This structure and its maintenance is understood to be the perceived authority of the identity. It is as important for the internal workings of the organisation as it is for those on the outside, for if this visual representation of status and power is clearly understood, it communicates an inescapable sense of direction and order.

Thought—the establishment of order is a prerequisite for effective identity.

There are two issues here: firstly, a visual display of command and, secondly, whether this necessarily mirrors the true nature of the organisation being identified.

An organisation can, should it choose to do so, group its visual appearance together, so that all its operations are encompassed and displayed in the same manner, and therefore recognised as one collective entity. This does not just apply to a single individual or organisation with a small range of products destined for the same market. It can also apply to larger, more complex organisations or groups which may serve several unconnected markets. Here the repercussions of being seen to serve unconnected markets and activities may or may not be beneficial. Being perceived as large or small, specialist or multidisciplinary may have a direct influence upon how these markets react to their presence.

These decisions should usually be based upon the demands of the market, unless you decide to go for an opportunity to redefine a market rather than dumbly following its demands. Meanwhile, strong forces and personalities within an organisation can lead to calls for devolution or takeover between rival divisions, product bases and brands. However, despite these occasional pressures, the litmus test must rule. How will the market respond? Will it share your motivation and reward you accordingly, or be confused, non-plussed or alienated by the identity structure you present it with?

Before an audience can learn to disbelieve, they will tend to accept the pattern they see. A sceptical audience is one which has learnt the failings of a structure. That is providing they can understand it. The system and hierarchy of the identity being presented is one of the main underlying patterns upon which they will develop their toler-ance of and trust in an organisation, its apparent values, authority, distribution, ownership and—should it have any—parent organis-ations, subsidiaries and divisions, product families and brands.

The larger an organisation's activities, the more vital it is to pay close attention to a properly considered and maintained identity structure. Frequently, an otherwise well-organised business is made to appear foolish by mismanagement of this kind. This isn't just about an expanding business losing its clarity. It also applies to those who, by ignorance of their identity structure, shoot themselves in the foot, not uncommonly with irreversible consequences.

A structure begins its development around the name of the organi-sation, its subsidiaries, divisions, product ranges and brands. The visual linkages between these need consideration. Each has a rela-tionship to be negotiated by the identity. There are differing levels—hierarchical issues to be resolved for the viewer. Some elements wish or need to be publicised more assertively than others. Some ele-ments may need to endorse others, whilst some deny or have need to compete with one another. Some elements may even have need to remain obscure or anonymous. The centralised or decentralised relationship between these activities and their names and brands dictates the most suitable structure of identity.

There are two clearly defined structures of identity to choose from: a Mono-identity or a Multi-identity. Between these two exists a grey area, largely extended and managed by endorsement, or mismanaged, in which case the notion of structure is lost altogether.

Mono-identity

This is a single visual style for an organisation: one which permeates all its operations and products. A Mono-identity punches its full weight in a single direction, for every element within the identity— and therefore the entire organisation—is clearly seen to support the whole. There is no conflict or competition of values because the structure of the identity speaks with one centralised voice. Because of its apparent simplicity, it seems to be the easiest and most economical structure to manage, but it requires a clarity and discipline few are equipped to maintain.

This category of identity structure can be extended to subsidiaries, divisions and products, but only within the boundaries of remaining a single and clearly understood verification of the central identity. It must still be seen as a totality, even though some relaxation or addition of style may be authorised for semi-autonomous or independent subsidiaries or marketing operations. These fringes mark the beginnings of weakness, for the immaculate hallmark of a Mono-identity is its implicit authority, made possible by its continuous and regulated visual discipline and procedure.

Illustration 12

Mono-identity

This is a single name and visual style, one which permeates all the products
and operations of an organisation.

Parent
organisation

Subsidiaries
or Divisions

Products
and Services

Illustration 13

Multi-identity

This is a collection of different names and visual styles applied to different aspects of the organisation, its products and services.

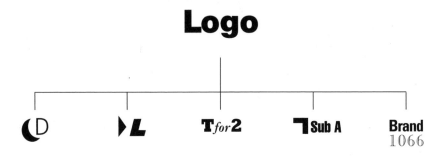

If these same logos are rearranged, this time without the lines denoting the family tree, there is no longer any clue to their relationship.

Multi-identity

As the name implies, this is the co-existence of more than one identity or brand. It is often suitable for fast-moving or transient operations where it is useful for the identity of the product to remain autonomous from the parent organisation. Alternatively it may be a result of acquisition, perhaps several companies operating in different sectors—sometimes competitors under the same owner-ship—all of which enjoy a status and goodwill derived from their existing identities and can see no added value in relinquishing them. They may or may not link to one another by endorsement. The strength with which these differing identities bind together can vary widely. Different divisions or products may appear to be related or unrelated according to whatever degree of closeness suits their current or long-term objectives.

One way of looking at this is to imagine a Multi-identity as the hull of an ocean liner designed with several bulkheads or compartments of division. Each compartment can appear self-sufficient, should it choose. Dependant upon the level of this interaction or apparent freedom is the risk-management of fashion, experimentation and failure because, though through accident a bulkhead may fail, the effect of this need not necessarily flood or damage its neighbours. The ship of the organisation should remain afloat, its overall objectives unimpeded, providing the design and integrity of the structure and the skill with which it is managed permit it to do so. If managed successfully, the survival of one identity need not rely upon another. The additional benefits of this approach can be the capability of catering for multiple or fast-moving markets in a manner considered neither suitable nor possible for the parent organisation to be seen to be involved in.

The benefit and cost of this independence is a dilution of the perceived overall scale of an organisation's efforts and operations. The focus and return of resources diverges: the audience of one sector may remain unaware of the links of ownership (and therefore the possible connection of values) between the main identity of each individual identity.

The idea is to play this game in order to achieve benefit. An organisation may even set one division or sector and its brands in competition with another—a fabricated contest for the audience, perhaps going as far as to deny the relationship between the two. The politics of emphasis between the endorsed and the endorsee can vary according to historical and current need, the opportunities being sought, and the legality of the action and circumstances.

Each identity may be founded upon different values or intangibles. These may remain separate from those of the controlling organisation, and managed through their unique combination of firmwords, with as many subsets as required. This is a decentralised identity structure with identity management protecting a variety of diverse and fragmented areas of operation.

The extreme manifestation of a Multi-identity is complete non-endorsement. This is where the parent organisation and its subsidiaries visually divide to such an extent that they deliberately do not refer to one another. Here the identities of each brand appear to be entirely unconnected with one another.

Choice and maintenance

If you are a fledging operation, the choice may not seem relevant. The initial extent of your activities, products or services may not appear to need any particular awareness of structure. Yet the moment you voluntarily begin to expand your operations—or the demand is placed upon you to do so—the strains of visual confusion caused by a lack of co-ordination appear. So it pays to be aware of both current and anticipated structure.

The choice or maintenance of a Multi-identity structure offers flexibility and the comfort of marketing experimentation, with no loss of face should all not proceed as planned. It may be considered worthwhile developing a distinct individualistic identity for each market with less regard for the temporary or permanent nature of the opportunity each market presents. If so, a Multi-identity offers a changeable and selective visual umbrella of support; individual products can be endorsed or denied at will by the reputation, name and identity of the parent organisation or brand. As a result, there may be several identities to be developed, maintained and trusted by several audiences. The complexities of this obviously demand a corresponding effort and allocation of resources.

Alternatively, the structure of a Mono-identity offers a fixed visual umbrella of total support. Here, each product is endorsed by the reputation, name and identity of the parent organisation. There is only one identity to be promoted, maintained and trusted. As a result, it has the most forceful power-to-weight ratio of identity in terms of the trade-off between effort and reward. The downside for some is that it relies on total concentration, for should any component of the identity suffer, it is the entire identity that pays the price.

The permutations are endless. Often an organisation suddenly needs to combine the two structures, maintaining a mono approach for its key identity whilst promoting a set of unconnected multiple identities elsewhere.

Illustration 14

A Mono-identity extended over too contradictory a range of market activities.

A Mono-identity retains its credibility and central authority through the smallest of linkages. These connections can be fragile and susceptible to breakage, mistreatment or abuse. If the growing nature of the organisation it represents is allowed to extend itself over too disparate a range of market activities, and where the existing identity struggles to successfully combine this new market diversity, the identity begins to flounder. A Mono-identity cannot be seen to contradict itself. Beware in case you do not see the contradiction as quickly or clearly as your audience. This is a major danger area for a Mono-identity—the unbridgeable gulf or potential abyss whereupon an identity begins to satisfy itself more than the needs of its audience. It is before you reach this point that the restructuring of the identity or else the curtailment of an over-extended or incongruous mixture of market operations must be addressed.

Illustration 15

If these three organisations (or divisions of an organisation) insist on sharing the same Mono-identity, it must be because they are placing their own self-importance before the needs of their audiences.

One type of organisation susceptible to this problem is one whose management wishes to move faster than the audience either expects or wishes; and perhaps also too fast for the existing identity to keep up with. Entrepreneurs often build or acquire businesses in such a way, with great success or failure. Their difference is, hopefully, that they fully realise their continued success depends on their wits, and probably no one else's. They rely on their instincts being in tune with what may always be a fickle and disparate set of audiences. The failure occurs when they leave, or the visual distance between each manifestation of the same identity no longer succeeds in making any sense to the audience.

Mono-identities also fail through the gradual or sudden introduction of disparate, irrelevant or incomprehensible patterns of graphics into the centre of their key areas of identity. A Mono-identity thrives on consistency—and those linkages and the intangible values that underpin them must never be compromised, visually fragmented or dissolved by the use of any unsuitable or contradictory signals. Again, if the management fails to understand the identity structure they are operating within, the identity is out of control. The audience, commonly having no notion of what identity structure even is, nevertheless instinctively realises that this particular identity is losing form, discipline and focus. Furthermore, they may even interpret these changes to the identity as a form of devolution; a weakening of the centre. In this way the structural authority of the identity has been challenged, if not destroyed, and credibility delivered a blow it may take a long while to recover from. Meanwhile, perhaps, in the background, investors may be puzzled by the trading losses, not necessarily connecting this event with the structural identity blunder.

Dressing up, dressing down

If an identity structure is the framework, what dress sense do you decorate this framework with? How you 'dress' your identity structure reflects your awareness of etiquette. Personality, or certainly an excess of it, can undermine an identity if it is not contained within a suitable framework of expression. In other words, it needs to be neatly ringfenced, so it may freely occur only within well-defined areas.

For example, some markets may demand formal dress, such as traditionally tailored suits, but the wearers can still express a glimpse of their personality through their choice of dress accessories. In the same manner a tactical military aircraft can express the personality of its aircrew within a limited display area, perhaps allowing for a small personal illustration or motif. Within such clearly demarcated areas, these flashes of personality can be as individualistic as is wished. Because they are countered and strictly surrounded by the order of the overall identity, and clearly seen to be so, they can be understood, tolerated and expected. They do not challenge the overall identity structure.

These examples of containing personality merely make the point that dress sense, in its broadest sense, means dressing for the occasion. There are both casual and formal situations and markets within which an identity must necessarily operate. Some promotional work may demand a more relaxed attitude or indication of casual style. Some items, such as a 'fun pack' designed to appeal to child passengers on an airline, obviously need to communicate at child level, yet also still appear to be belonging to and authorised by the overall identity. Therefore an amusing or informal approach may be appreciated by all, adults and children alike.

But should this same air carrier allow its aircraft livery to dress down too far, it may challenge its audience's notion of occasion as well as structure. Formality relates in part to preparation and seriousness. The preparation of aircraft for safe flight is a highly regulated procedure. Therefore, if the graphics challenge this sense of strict order and formality through the use of excessively casual graphics, the result may be deemed to be a contradiction of signals too far.

The point is that dress sense should be correctly applied and managed, however spontaneous it may occasionally need to appear.

Your dress code must work within the structure of your identity. It should also adhere to your firmwords. If you deny or misunderstand these basic factors operating beneath your identity, you will end up making mistakes.

Logo

Why have a logo?

Identity demands that you must have a name if you wish to be identified. To communicate this name involves telling and showing: it must be used verbally and must almost certainly appear on display material. The manner in which you are seen is therefore the manner in which you may be judged.

By design or default, an organisation must present its name in a given style, and if it then wishes to regulate this and, with deliberation, add further communication to its presentation, it must design and control this procedure. Through the use of particular typefaces or graphics a name elevates itself to a logo.

Through modern usage, the word 'logo' has come to mean a symbol, a name set in a distinctive typographical style, or a combination of both. A logo communicates with intent to stir emotion, which it should do with a simple ease—simply notable, simply understandable—and, for ease of reproduction, simply reproducible.

A logo represents. The best provide potent and immediate communication in order to gain recognition, promote a particular set of values and act as endorsement for the bearer.

Ironically, despite the simplicity of the best logos, the more successful they become, the more they may defy conscious recognition, if you doubt this, attempt to draw some famous logos familiar to you, but without any reference. Unless you are exceedingly visually intelligent, you may be surprised at how difficult this task is. Yet even if you fail to visualise the detail of these logos, when you next see them you will, of course, recall them in a flash. What you recall is a certain instant, and it is at this point that the logo is doing its job as both representative and endorser for the other information which may surround it. It acts as a conduit for the rest of the identity.

Thought—the best logos play upon the unconscious mind.

This is the ideal. However, logos often achieve much less, confusing or thwarting both the viewer and wearer. Some demand too much conscious attention, the viewer becoming distracted by their construction or the significance of meaning. Often, there is not enough quality to match or penetrate the imagination of the viewer. Attention can easily stumble or halt altogether with the logo alone through its failure to lead the viewer beyond itself. A logo should infer that it represents something of significance and interest, a direction or subject worth following, something more than the sum of itself. If the logo fails to endorse anything beyond or fails to introduce you to a wider sense of identity, its mission is weak, if not futile. This is why an effective identity cannot just rely upon a logo and nothing else. Equally, a logo should never 'give it all away' on first meeting by furnishing too much detail—trying to convey more information than it should be expected to indicate. It is a virtuous element that should rightly refuse to gratify too much too soon. It exists to signpost: it is the signal placed to beckon the viewer to think or believe beyond their current situation.

A bad logo is one which appears lifeless or exhausted. It either tries too hard or fails to try enough. It is ill conceived and uncoordinated, inept for the method of reproduction, wrong size, inappropriate colour, typeface and message; no logo at all may for many organisations be an improvement.

A logo should promote with clarity the correct values. It is no good getting attention for the wrong reasons or misleading the viewer by promising one thing, yet delivering another. It should promise the truth, or else it might fail through being 'found out'. Like any other aspect of an identity, it must adhere to the correct values of the product or organisation—the intangibles that propel the identity at its best.

Endorsement by logo

Another role of a logo is to endorse the correct values of all the other messages, written or graphic, which surround it. The logo is a central point around which all other messages must be fastened. Ultimately, the act of endorsing is its prime task, the role it will live or die by.

Thought—who is endorsing whom, what is endorsing what?

An identity is the interface between physical reality and emotional reality: what is and what is presented. The logo needs to endorse all within this dimension. But what dimension is this exactly? Has any-one bothered to map out its territory? You should do, for the law of this area of operation will be the structure of the identity, the method of interface to be employed—Mono-identity or Multi-identity, as discussed in the previous chapter. These choices are to be made before a designer can fruitfully be given the task of designing the logo itself. Before a logo can achieve anything beyond the confines of the organisation, it must address and endorse the law internally. The type and method of endorsements used must match the type and method of the identity structure best suited to the objectives of the organisation. Planning this structure beforehand saves remedial work later. To reconstruct a logo after the initial launch is an expensive and inconvenient exercise. While the recon-struction work gets underway, the strength of the identity is tem-porarily weakened—the castle walls can be breached and the progress of the organisation delayed.

An identity requires the capability to grow, change or alter to suit the climate it must survive within.

Firstly, your logo endorses you. Secondly, it endorses your values in accordance with your firmwords. Thirdly, it provides the mechanism for endorsing and communicating the nature of your organisation—centralised or decentralised, subsidiary, product, service or any other activity—internally and externally.

Logo variations

Thought—are you using the correct category of logo for your identity?

This depends upon your definition of the word 'logo'. Like many words connected to identity, it is not used with enough thought. A 'logo' means only an emblem or device used as the badge of an organisation in display material—in other words, a symbol. Yet there are a number of logo variations, differences which are seldom noted, but differences nonetheless which have wide-ranging implications through the restrictions and opportunities they offer.

The answer may be that a symbol in addition to your name may be the last thing you need. The logo variant correct for you depends upon a number of factors, but certainly you should not rush into any early assumptions about what you believe you need until you have planned your identity structure.

Logos can be broadly classified as two main variants:

- Logotype—a name in a particular typestyle
- Symbol—a badge or emblem.

In addition there are three others:

- Combined—a combined logotype and symbol
- Integral—an integrated logotype and symbol
- Virtual—a virtual logo, or icon.

The logotype

A logotype is a grouping of initials, a word or group of words which together form a name. It becomes a logotype, with a status beyond simply a name, when it is seen to be consistently used in a defined typeface, either a standard or customised font. It can often be plain in appearance, though the typeface may be the subject of some additional graphic treatment, the objective being to add to or accentuate the meaning or inferred value of the name. Another technique is to partially, or entirely, frame the name with a border design intended to strengthen its appearance and defendable space.

A logotype is self-contained in so far as it is capable of use without the need for any other separate symbol or device.

These three sample logotypes below depict a plain logotype with no decoration, a logotype with some simple graphic treatment and, finally, a logotype (in this example, plain) with a border device. Any graphics added to a logotype should conform to, and certainly not contradict, the values of the firmwords selected for the identity.

Illustration 16

Logotype

Logotype

Thought—logotypes are potent when the name or names they contain also have potency.

If your name is already understood to be synonymous with the qualities you wish to promote, or is already significantly established in
the minds of your audience—or promises to be so—you probably
require the simplicity and understatement of a logotype.

Some benefits of a logotype include the following:

■ A logotype is simple to execute.

■ Logotypes can be more readily designed to appear understated,
inferring a certain self-worth and confidence. For those assuming
a royal or personal status, you may even want to avoid any
display font whatsoever—the inference being that anyone who
needs to know knows already: ideal for social climbers and polite
personal letter headings. This attitude goes with never printing
your name under your signature on a letter: if you are that
important, why double the emphasis or show off more than you
need to?

■ A logotype concentrates attention upon the value of the name
itself. This is best if the values of the name are obviously well
known, such as an already famous brand or a name intended to
be publicised as pretending to be so.

■ A logotype is suitable if the character of the name is more pertinent or memorable than any worthwhile symbol could improve
upon, given the circumstances—indeed, it might be the case that
any additional symbolism would weaken the status of the name.

■ A logotype is ideal if you are so heavily endorsed by another, or
others—Royal Warrant, parent company or group, strength of
location, personality, celebrity or other company or product—
that a plain logotype is the option least likely to interfere with
any other graphics which must surround you.

■ Choose a logotype for reasons of dignity: if symbolism appears
to 'try too hard', or is suggestive of poor taste. You may not

choose to advertise what you would rather wish to remain private or exclusive; for example, an elite club may not want to be seen beyond its limited target audience. The potential low-key nature of a logotype can be a deliberate camouflage.

- If name alone is the most vital ingredient to your marketing efforts, for example the www or any other information directory.

- If the name is a brand or subsidiary of a larger group endorsed by another symbol—a situation where more than one symbol would be inappropriate.

- Where clarity of message is urgent: a legal instruction or process of law, or perhaps a foreign name where there is a need to spell it out in full. A clever logotype design is an opportunity to benefit from the otherwise difficult spelling or pronunciation of a name by concentrating attention upon it.

- For a personal or family name. Or the name of a personality whose character benefits from a direct or simple approach.

- If you cannot think of anything else, either because it is not necessary to compete with others, or you haven't the ability or budget to do anything else well enough.

All identities must generally include a logotype, for the name always needs communication. Whether you also require a symbol depends upon the nature of your name, as well as your organisation, audience, values and structure of identity.

Beyond the simple treatment of type, a logotype can be decorated with other graphics. The purpose of this decoration must be to invent something unique: first by choice or invention of typeface, secondly by suggestion or accentuation of intangibles or a message within the name. This may be achieved by transforming one or more of the characters, or adding other non-type-specific elements, such as a border, rules, shape, illustration or other symbolism.

The most common solutions contain these graphics as an integral part of the logotype. However, if the graphics become a symbol separate from the logotype, you need to consider whether they should always be combined with the logotype—in other words, working as a fixed unit or a symbol capable of working independently.

Using both a logo (symbol) and logotype together has its benefits, especially for those who need to control a large, complex organisation; however, if your name constitutes a valuable asset, why distract or divert attention away from it with the addition of a separate symbol? It may be useful to have the two devices, but think this through carefully. The meaning and reason behind employing them, and the demarcation and system of usage, must produce a tangible benefit, or else it may weaken your identity by diverting attention away from the inherent status of the name.

The symbol

A symbol is a badge that does not include a name. It is designed to stand alone or, on occasion, combine with an otherwise separate logotype. Because it contains no meaningful wordage, its effectiveness to communicate is dependent upon how recognisable it is to the intended audience. Often a symbol may have formerly been combined with a logotype but through common usage, or notoriety, became capable of communicating effectively without the need for the actual logotype to be included. Recognising the symbol infers a common understanding, or even membership, for, with no name, its fame or obscurity may suit its purpose—perhaps the badge of a local club, an entire nation. A symbol is capable of promoting the privacy or exclusivity of its membership. Elect to use a symbol with care in case it appears to an audience as a signal of vanity; many organisations crave a symbol when in fact they do not require one. This is a common failure of identity.

Symbols work best for large operations, especially product-based businesses whose common presence of branded physical products constitutes the main visual manifestation of the organisation: for example, an automobile manufacturer or a company whose consistency of delivery, service or output alludes to being that of a virtual product—such as the inherent and often branded attitude or methods adopted by some institutions which also enjoy an element of personal membership. This includes schools, political movements, fund-raising charities, clubs or other networks or areas of operation. A symbol, being a message for the initiated, works in sectors with limited display areas such as fashion clothing and other articles of decoration where the subtlety of a symbol without name promotes a partnership between the communicator and the audience recognising it. To do this successfully, the symbol must be simple enough to work with printing techniques and have an aspect ratio capable of severe reduction in size—as an extreme example, if used as a decoration on a cuff link.

These three sample logos depict a series of symbols. The first contains the initial 'L' but in such an abstract way it is not necessarily recognisable as such.

A symbol is useful because:

■ It uses no written language and therefore requires no translation.

■ In theory, it is capable of severe size reduction—often beyond the potential of a logotype.

■ It can remain identifiable from a greater distance, whereas a logotype at the same distance may be more difficult to 'read'.

■ It can be quickly recognised—making it ideal for mass markets.

■ It can readily be used to endorse another organisation or product logo, often with no need for any additional logotype.

Symbols mirror the history of mankind. The opportunities to create a truly original design are limited. Though you should attempt to have a more optimistic attitude than this, you must remain vigilant in case the symbolism you use either clashes, offends or has had its meaning hijacked by association with an existing or historical movement, organisation, shape, pattern or colour.

The combined logo

A logo can take the form of a combined logo: a symbol and logotype as two separate items but positioned together in order to form a single working unit.

In a combined logo the symbol tends to act as an endorsement of the logotype—perhaps a sign of guarantee or mark of true or pretended prestige. As with all graphics that form part of any logo, the meaning can be literal, suggestive or even purely decorative, but it must always be in tune with the firmwords of the identity.

A combined logo is useful when:

■ A logotype is in need of more suggested prestige.

■ A name has, or pretends to, a history.

■ Different logotypes need to be endorsed by the same symbol.

An example of a combined logo:

A combined logo can be employed to endorse another organisation or (as in this example, with an optional change of colour) the logo-type of a product:

The integral logo

An integral logo is a symbol which contains a logotype within its own boundaries, as the example below shows.

This has all of the attributes of being a symbol, yet also contains the name. This form of logo is a highly effective medium where certain benefits of using a symbol are most relevant to your needs but you also wish to use the name because it has a quality or value of com-munication worthy of retention at all times.

The name should ideally be generic enough to work more or less regardless of differences in language and culture. It is also helpful if that name is short enough for the purposes of the symbol to remain effective when being reduced to a small size.

An integral logo is useful when:

■ The name has some merit but requires added strength.

■ There is the need for greater opportunity or application of graphics (beyond the possibilities offered within just the logotype).

- Small size reproduction is important.

- A logo as a badge has obvious uses.

- When endorsing another organisation or product logo.

An integral logo can be employed (with a varying degree of prominence) to endorse another product or (as in this example) the logo-type of another organisation:

The virtual logo

A virtual logo occurs when a product ultimately becomes so established within the broader realms of society that it becomes in effect an icon in its own right. In other words, though possibly badged, the product has little need for the application of a logo. The product is self-defining and self-sustaining, exercising more power than the original pretend brand. It has become a real brand.

This is not necessarily a rare destiny. If the product has enough reputation to stand alone and be instantly recognised, it can be used as a virtual logo—it may supersede the need for the logo because its photographic image at the base of an advertisement substitutes. In this way it can act as a 'sign-off, pretending to 'say it all', especially when combined with a supporting qualification.

Picture of
product

The Original. Since 1983.

Relationships

The need to endorse and the mechanics of doing so help to decide the ideal identity structure and choice of logo variants. All these elements need to co-operate or an identity becomes confusing, if not ultimately lawless.

Beyond these elements are the relationships which further assist in explaining the nature of the organisation or product being identified: the relationships between the different components of an identity. These relationships are visual signals which explain who owns, endorses, befriends or authorises whom. For example, a holding company may need to display its relationship with a subsidiary, an organisation with a product, and one brand with another.

Parent and child

One way of managing these relationships is to see them as parent and child relationships. A parent may choose to display its relationship between itself and its offspring. The level of dominance or control the parent is seen to exercise over the child can vary. This is where the logo variant of the parent organisation becomes critical. It dictates the boundaries within which the relationship can be visually managed.

 **Subsidiary** A

 **Product** A

An integrated or symbol parent logo adapts very easily, as the above two examples show.

However, a logotype or combined parent logo where the design does not lend itself easily to being split into separate symbol and logotype (for example, the symbol is so commonplace a graphic as to be rendered meaningless without the logotype supporting it) poses a different set of problems, as shown below.

Here, the parent logo, willingly or otherwise, tends to compete with the child, unless countered by differences in scale between the two, which makes the suggested relationship obvious to the audience.

Matters can be clarified by the addition of other explanations.

But the addition of two apparently unrelated logos plants confusion and indicates a nervous parent or child.

If the two logos are seen to be equal, they enter the consenting adult category.

Logotype   **Logo**type

The partnership between the two logos may not be clear unless explained. Are they together by choice or not? Are they equals which together form one unit—such as a consortium? You may insist that you are equals, yet cynical audiences will always seek to guess which is the dominant partner. Such relationships need to be handled with great sensitivity.

If the relationship is more specific, again you will need to qualify the partnership.

Brand-A
——AT——
Logotype

In general, the public approval or endorsement between a parent and child works in both directions. A child can benefit from the status or heritage of its parent, sharing the reputation of the parent where the audit trail or genealogy is both useful and appealing to the target audience.

Qualifications

A logo is a form of self-qualification. You have branded yourself, and this logo advertises you both in person and in your absence.

In addition to the relationships of any parent organisation or affiliated brand exists the management of other self-awarded qualifications and selling points such as location, age and other explanations, temporary or semi-permanent badges or supporting lines of text. Also the licence, endorsement or other seal of approval by an independent source may qualify you.

■ Geography

Logo • LONDON

■ Age

Logo • ESTABLISHED 1835

■ Subject or product area

Logo • MENSWEAR

■ Values or call to action

Logo • JOIN THE NETWORK NOW

■ Personality

Logo • AS WORN BY *Lowe*

■ Point of contact

Logo • TELEPHONE 123 4567

Logos are not limited to having only one type of relationship or qualification—they can be mixed and matched in order to suit your purpose and audience, as the following examples show:

Logo • GO ON... SAY IT • www.firmwords.com

[royal seal] **Logo** • OF BOND STREET

Logo • UK • ENGINEERING

Logo of England • FROM 1902

NEW Logo • RELIEF FROM HEADACHES

Logo • MATURE CHEDDAR • TASTE THE DIFFERENCE

Trust Logo *to always get it right!*

`Logo` • PARIS—ROME—NEW YORK

`Logo` • WORLDWIDE • www.markrowden.com

`Logo` • 24 HOURS • www.firmwords.com

WELCOME TO `Logo` **WORLD**

Qualifications act as both limitations and advantages. Establish them with care, giving clear instructions for their integration with your logo. Enshrine these instructions as a clearly explained part of your identity guidelines. Specify typefaces, sizes and positioning details so as to ensure a uniform appearance. If you fail to make the rules clear, these 'add-on' elements will look just that: random and ill-considered, reducing the effectiveness and authority of your logo. Any additional elements which appear alongside your logo should be marshalled to appear as a deliberate and fully intended, autho-rised integral statement.

In the area of audiovisual communications, these qualifications may be delivered verbally or by animation, but of course they still form part of your identity. So, again, care must be taken for the sake of consistency and integrity.

You should try to recognise the expected lifespan of the qualifications you intend to use—some may match the lifespan of the identity, but most will fade through use over a shorter period. Distinguishing the timeless from the transient is a key element of qualification management. Beware, for what you may judge today as being permanent or transient may tomorrow suddenly veer in the opposite direction. An additional phrase can become more notable than the rest of the identity, perhaps a catchphrase—for better or worse. Alternatively, and sometimes overnight, it can become your worst nightmare.

Any qualification or relationship between your identity and logo and another more temporary element can over time marginalise the identity, rendering it entrenched with a set of values you may not have anticipated or planned for. An identity can so easily become stuck because of its associations and qualifications. Likewise, published statements of policy and opinion or the associations with the newly famous or infamous can quickly overtake you. For example, a scandal breaks about a personality paid to endorse you, or something you say about yourself, even a casual aside, suddenly comes, through the connivance of fate, to appear dangerously negative. If you recognise marginalisation too late, the relationship or qualification may trap and seal the fate of your identity. If this fate is unacceptable, you must extract yourself at the first warning sign, or your promoted relationship or qualification will forever share the same lifespan as your product, short or long lived. This encapsulation may seal you into only one area of activity or history. You thereafter become the victim of novelty or fashion cycles.

It is more common for a qualification to hijack an identity than many suppose. For example, a startlingly successful supporting phrase, strapline or memorable jingle can on occasion overtake in importance and recognition the brand itself, the most notable successes becoming what they promised: memorable, for better or worse, long after the change of direction or possible demise of the brand.

These additional qualifications are like the 'extras' you add to a production to make it more spectacular, attractive or believable. They add extra dimension, impact or scale to your presentation. If you manage them as though they are extras, you will not go wrong. The trouble can arise when such an extra shines so brilliantly from its originally intended support role that it starts to steal the show. In particular a catchphrase which through its very success steals the limelight of the show, in this case the product or organisation. Whilst to begin with this extra impact and resulting attention may be welcomed, over time it may gradually begin to sidetrack the other things you would, by then, rather be saying, like an old performing artist wishing to perform new tunes with an audience which won't let them escape their former success, insisting instead on hearing the 'old favourites'.

So, before the beneficial effect of a qualification assumes too much permanence, it may be prudent to introduce a replacement qualification to maintain the mobility of the identity. If you do not react in time, it becomes increasingly difficult to make the change. And remain aware that change is likely to be necessary before the point when the audience tells you.

Colour

The nature of colour

Everything within our world displays itself by the use of colour. In tone, texture, light and shade, natural colours, both iridescent and delicate in tone, surround us. These colours of the natural world appear to have reason or purpose—and certainly beauty. Likewise, the colours you use for an identity should have similar reason, purpose and empathy with the objectives of your identity.

Colour is emotive. It represents many values, including age. For every graduation from the light of day to the dark of night—from white to black and every tone between—signals the season and time of day. The age of some colours indicates precise periods of history: a particular year, decade or century. Many colours available today were not obtainable in the past. Invention and advances in colour technology have greatly expanded the range of colours available, as well as the material upon which they can be successfully reproduced. This expansion of colour has changed our perception of it. For example, the colour white has changed as technology has advanced. Formerly a vellum or creamy consistency, modern whites are capable of much greater brightness. For this reason the apparent age, and therefore tone, of white (or any other colour) used on behalf of an identity should be chosen with care, or else run the risk of contradicting the age values of the identity.

The vitality of bright colours tends to suggest youth and an optimism towards the future, whilst darker tones often appear to indicate maturity and values established in the past.

Pastels, an alternative to bright or sombre colours, by their softness of tone blur the boundaries of age and much more. Compared to 'solid' colours, they appear gentle, yet indefinite. This may suit some applications but be positively wrong in others, as for a warning sign which needs to be more visible and precise in its instruction.

Fashion is also a major factor when selecting colours. Certain tones, with only occasional slight variations, remain fashionable over very long periods, whilst others arrive like shooting stars, vividly announcing themselves overnight only to burn out just as quickly. Whilst they remain in vogue it seems that such colours can do no wrong, suggesting they might sell any product, regardless of its other attributes of quality.

Neutral tones offer the greatest security from the ravages of fashion, though their prominence in the league tables of style will still vary. The great benefit of neutrals is their ability to support and complement a wide range of other colours.

Colour variation

If colour heralds age, it also belongs to location. Different cultures have developed their own native colours. Some colours and palettes of colours are capable of reminding us of certain locations—Indian or 'Red Indian', French, British, African, Caribbean, and many more.

A colour looks different depending upon the lighting conditions under which it is viewed. Light from a normal electric bulb tends to be red, whereas light from a fluorescent tube tends to be blue. For this reason, it is recommended that all colours, where possible, should be viewed in a good neutral light such as natural daylight. The colour of daylight also varies enormously according to the climate, time of day and moisture in the atmosphere. The same blue held in the natural light of the Mediterranean appears quite differently when displayed in the natural light of another area or continent.

How a colour is seen also depends on the substance and expanse of the coloured surface being viewed. A large surface area tends to reflect more light, therefore lightening the colour, whilst a smaller surface area tends to darken a colour.

Colours react differently when mixed, mismatched, combined or contrasted with each other. In simple terms, opposite colours improve one another, whilst others struggle to complement each other with varying degrees of success.

Colour management

Basic colour management—knowledge of the mechanics of colour together with at least some general idea of colour psychology—is a necessary skill for all those involved in identity design and management. This is because businesses in general are placed in the position of both receiving and offering their audiences complex messages and choices through the use of colour. Colour travels at the speed of light. What you say, or how pleasing something is to touch, taste or smell, arguably lags along behind this first sensation. For most this is both undeniable and unavoidable. Those unfortunate enough to be blind escape this confusion, instead beginning their exploration of the other senses first—just as confusing though they may be. Whatever your sense preference, to be able to justify the colours you use and quantify their effect is to be in control of a major component of your identity. In addition, your skill in evaluating the colour schemes of other identities will be just as useful.

Often the choices people make are by persuasion of colour alone. Sometimes a manufacturer may either guide or restrict the colour choice available, with good intention. A range of products may be suited best to a small range of colours or colour combinations.

Restricting this to the only choices available ensures control of taste and identity—their identity, the identity of the product and the purchaser's identity. A poor colour choice detracts from the marketplace identity and value of the product being sold, as well as the pleasure of the customer. If the longevity of a product also means it will be advertising your identity twenty-five years from now, this form of control is advisable.

Thought—the use colour is not necessarily good for your health.

Certainly not all colours suit you—either on a personal dress level or as an organisation. The influence of colour cannot be underestimated. Our personal likes and dislikes form a map in our minds of what appeals and that which we would rather avoid. Some people are more colour-sensitive than others. Conscious of our colour preferences or not, we all make, or are subjected to, a daily bombardment of colour choices at home, work or play, as our home decor, office, automobiles and clothing all testify.

Some colours calm whilst others excite: for example, a red interior for a passenger aircraft would seem less suitable than a calm blue. In a sports car, the excitement of red may be desirable. As a gentleman, a pink evening suit may be the most desirable item in your wardrobe or the most unlikely. What is true is that some colours (and, it should be said, textures, shapes and patterns) produce sharp differences in opinion, whilst the appeal or acceptance of others remain less controversial. Certain colours may be acceptable amongst only a narrow range of the particular audience you are addressing, for taste in colour is so often a signal of membership. Signal your acceptance of the status quo or renounce it by controversial use of colour; whether the choice is unwittingly or deliberate, the effect is likely to be the same.

Colours are often associated with a certain product or production method. Such products often enjoy a history, originating from a region or other cultural area. The links to these customary colour schemes may be more deep-rooted than you estimate. If you choose to turn your back on this custom or heritage, only do so by adopting that which will offer you significant improvement or advantage.

Select your colour schemes through a process of thought and elimination. The truth is that of the thousands of colour shades available most can be dismissed for one reason or another. Firstly, many will be unsuited to your industry or marketplace. Others will need to be avoided for reasons of competition. All will need justifying in relation to your firmwords, combined with an acute understanding of your products or services.

For example, in Test 5 on page 68 some firmword combinations were shown. Taking just one combination of firmwords from the examples shown might produce the following train of discussion:

Geometry—Art : Active

These firmwords have been selected for a leading producer of computer-aided design software. These products are the most advanced available, providing a virtual reality display, with integrity, from the data programmed by the engineer or other creative operator. This data also produces detailed drawings and a raft of other essential information, including all component lists.

Active—certain colours in nature belong to activity, others to more static phenomena. The word 'active' demands colours bright or light enough to suggest the possibility of transformation or movement. In which case, chocolate brown would seem less mobile than beige, which would seem markedly less energetic or moving than a bright yellow, vivid blue, bright white or flame red. Certainly the products being promoted are aspiring to the future, rather than the safety of the past. 'Older' colours should be avoided. More forward-looking colours should be employed. Hence the call for active—a movement towards the future.

Geometry—applies to natural law, as we understand it. This may be interpreted as primary colours, colours to signify the underlying dynamics of nature. Alternatively, due to the abstract nature of higher mathematics, bright synthetic colours, indicative of leading-edge enquiry and experimentation, may on occasion fit. But these 'experimental colours' are unproven and, if this firmword relates to a discipline of proven law, would be unsuitable. This distinction would depend upon the nature of the organisation and products being identified and promoted. In this case, the integrity of the computer data is an essential attribute of the product. So any colour misrepresenting the ultimate truth or conclusion of a project, let us say an ambiguous colour, would be unsuitable.

Art—encompasses all the colours of a painter's palette. We would need to establish the nature of the painter's style. The other firmwords in this combination—*geometry* and *active*—suggest modern art rather than any other period or style. When one thinks of art and geometry, the artist Mondrian springs to mind. Again, bright and bold primary colours would suggest a confirmation of the suggested colours of *geometry*.

The nature of this exploration needs to be experienced within the realms of a real situation—organisation and product—so that the finer points of the argument can be seen in an accurate light. By this method suitable colours can be identified and experimented with in terms of proposed logo designs, typefaces, sample literature or other visuals. Even so, a degree of abstract reflection is required—a common process for professional designers to partake in, but not necessarily enjoyed by all. What should be clear is that there exists a framework for directing and containing worthwhile discussion and exploration about the values of some colours in preference to others. Without this desire to justify colour usage, you operate by your personal instincts, or the instincts of others, alone. Even if these instincts are enlightened, can you convey or share them consistently and rapidly with others who may also need to work on the project with you?

In this way, the use of colour and the decision-making process employed to justify it should be managed, rather than left alone, as they so commonly are.

Dimensions

Shape management

Shape both presents and hides bulk. It heralds the content it pretends to contain. It also alters the corresponding shapes of the space that must necessarily surround it.

The management of space, vacant or filled, is one of the prime considerations for an identity. This is because an identity marks the boundaries of an area, physically, psychologically, or both. These borders define market, areas of operation and the intangible values an identity proposes to promote or defend.

Thought—no borders, no definition, no difference.

If an identity releases an organisation or product to fulfil its true potential, it must also restrain the wearer from making errors in presentation. It must prevent the unsuitable style or content that they might otherwise unintentionally present. It is a filtration system through which the wearer's communication interacts with the outside world. And it better be fit for the job, for this means filtering the correct shape of thought, as well as physique. The frontiers formed may change over time, edging forwards or backwards to suit the climate of fashion, taste and the opportunity of new technology, but yet still remain a clearly labelled territory which needs defending. Unless you clearly signpost these territories, there is no identity. You have nothing tangible to protect or promote.

Test 9

You may remember these shapes from Test 1 on pages 6–7.
Now choose the shape which best describes your organisation.

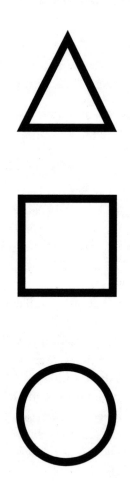

Only three shapes to choose from, but one will suit the intuitive personality and subject matter of your organisation more accurately than the others will. Whatever the choice, reflect upon your decision. Do not be surprised if the answer eludes you, for shape is a major root of emotional confusion. You may instinctively sense that one shape complements or reflects your nature better than another—and it will—but for many this is a difficult concept to acknowledge or articulate.

Thought—confusion is often a form of beautiful.

True beauty defies description. So often judged on shape alone, beauty confounds. It is this unresolved interplay upon the senses, rather than any other precise or understood specification, which fills the eye of the beholder.

Test 10

Taking a subject at random, for example the Internet, contemplate for a moment. Ask yourself what the Internet looks like.

Resist turning this page until you have decided on a shape.

Is this the Internet?

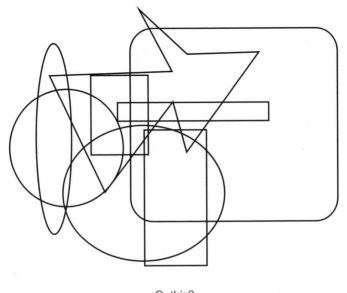

Or this?

Or an open space with no boundaries?

Shapes are suggestive. Each represents a differing 'truth', which calls for you to agree, passively accept or consciously dismiss. Whatever your opinion, the power of shape alone has challenged, manipulated or enhanced your thought process. It may have created a thought that otherwise would not exist. Perhaps, for you, your realisation of the shape of the Internet is infinity: the suggestion of no shape, just infinite size—a difficult concept for the human brain, and not helpful as an aid to the worldly aims of corporate identity. Perhaps no one has yet defined this space, or portion of it, which is what interests you. If you are an Internet service provider, perhaps you should attempt to do so before anyone else successfully claims what you may, mistakenly or otherwise, believe to be your territory.

Shape, especially when combined with colour, can offer the promise or suggestion of many other attributes such as gender, age, maturity, culture, fitness, vocation, function, subject, wealth, social status and much more.

'How' this is achieved is the domain of the creative and visual literate. 'Why' is a responsibility, which can be shared by all.

Illustration 17

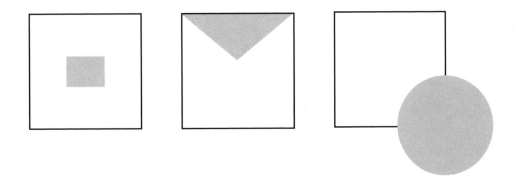

Within each of the above bordered rectangles the white spaces become as important a feature to the eye as the grey shaped infills.

Space, as well as size, significantly contributes to your identity. In any design or layout one shape fits within another. Even a blank page or display area is a shape. The gaps or interaction of the spaces between these shapes set the tone of pattern as well as the apparent tension, movement or stability of the design. Some ratios of size and space are more suited to your identity than others. You need to find the ideal measurements to suit your identity through experimentation or expert advice.

Thought—everything has an optimum size and position.

Every element can and should be positioned correctly. Correct position is instinctively understood once it is seen. However, arriving at an understanding of what makes the position of the elements in an identity correct takes great skill. The point is that some solutions work better than others. Just as some colours or shapes suit an identity more than others, size and position can also either work with perfect dynamics or only partially work, perhaps fooling long enough, satisfying enough, but most commonly denigrating the design and squandering the opportunities of achieving perfection. The rules for defining perfect size and position for the elements of your identity should, though not exclusively, concentrate on the logo. These rules should be an essential part of your final identity guidelines.

Often the perception of another's size rules people, perhaps to the point where they dare not challenge. This is because size is so often indicative of power. Yet what is presented may be far from the truth. Clever identity can minimise or exaggerate size at will. Therefore the accepted size of an organisation or product often needs to be become an issue of virtual reality.

Illustration 18

LOGO
not necessarily big

L   O   G   O
not necessarily small

Both size and inference of weight can suggest size.

Any audience may pass judgement on size before knowing any or all of the facts. They may well believe without challenge, which may either suit your aims or hinder them. Many stand fixated by the spell of an identity, both those who own it and those confronted by it, into a state of dumb compliance. Apparent size, whether real or fantastical, has a lot to do with confidence—the confidence to rule as well as challenge. For some this will also include the confidence to mislead—gently or greatly—for good reason or foul.

Thought—the power of an identity can seem infinite.

Big is not necessarily greater than small. Size of identity, in this context, means its cumulative effect in the minds of those who view it. This might depend upon twenty-four-hour, seven-day-a-week advertising or no promotion at all. It might be commonly available for all to see and understand, or else work quietly but diligently behind the scenes. The size of your marketplace may be immense or diminutive, but size of identity can operate independently of any physical reality. It does so by occupying, or better still, being invited into, the hearts and mind of your audience. The endless capacity for imagination means that size can therefore be infinite.

Illustration 19

Size is relative. Big or small, it is the grace with which you are seen to manage your space that creates the effect of size.

Illustration 20

Imagine that this different-sized logo is seen to appear on a variety of
badged products and marketing material. This imaginary logo appears
exactly to the same specification, but the sizes are erratic.

Logo   **Logo**   **Logo**

Logo   Logo   **Logo**

Logo   **Logo**   Logo

Logo   **Logo**   **Logo**

Logo   Logo   Logo

Logo   **Logo**   Logo

Logo   Logo   **Logo**

Illustration 21

Compared with the previous illustration, here is the same logo again, but with a system of regulated sizes.

Again, imagine that these different sizes are taken from a variety of badged products and marketing material. Notice the immense overall difference between the two illustrations.

Logo	Logo	Logo
Logo	Logo	Logo
Logo	Logo	Logo
Logo	Logo	Logo
Logo	Logo	Logo
Logo	Logo	Logo
Logo	Logo	Logo

Size of access

The regulation of space and size of access is, where practical, the restriction of the key elements of your identity to a series of fixed sizes. For example, limiting the size of a logo to few fixed-sized appearances regulates appearance. Although the management of this is likely to remain undetected by the audience, it creates a significantly higher level of consistency beyond the norm. Identity manages the choreography—its appearance as well as appearances. It is important to employ conditions of size and space wherever possible. In particular, use space as a ratio of understandable increments. This is where sophistication and consistency of pattern, as described earlier in this book, lend clarity and power. Just such simple management of size and disciplined level of consistency significantly increase the overall strength of an identity.

In more general terms, the use of size and the frequency of visibility with which an identity presents itself in a marketplace helps create the impression that others have about the willingness or wish of the organisation or product to be available. Consider whether the identity in question appears on every street corner, lives in a big house on the hill or is hidden in the back streets.

Illustration 22

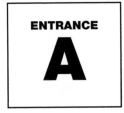 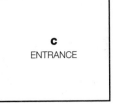

Three entrance signs. A speaks louder than B speaks louder than C.

Illustration 23

Another three signs, again all offering the same invitation, or do they? Consider the inflection of how much they appear to be both offering on the one hand and denying on the other.

Is the product which the identity promotes commonly available? Irregular or restricted availability or access might result in only limited publicity or recognition. The smaller organisation may lament this apparent limitation of promotion as the reason for any lack of success. Yet limited promotion or the uncommon can also mean exclusivity: if the identity, product and marketing affirm this in unison; and, if the self-confidence of the identity is both well founded and strong enough to refuse, or appear to refuse, business it does not desire. In other words, an identity is discerning, and shares this discrimination with its intended audience, those initiated, who in turn may also willingly allow a corresponding increase in your profit margins.

Thought—you locate, build and guard your access or accessibility.

Being available can be as counter-productive as being unavailable: both can drive you out of business. What your intended audience may prefer in relation to what is best for your objectives is a matter for you to decide. You can certainly be too available for your own good. You may have only one doorway to the street or, for that matter, the world, but if it is well considered, it may be the only entrance required. If you are offering a wide choice of entrances (telecommunicative or physical), ensure they are fully synchronised to your objectives and the desires of the audience you seek to serve. If not, stop wasting your time and theirs!

Consider how welcoming, purposeful or confusing these points of contact with your audiences are. They cannot be studied often enough. Closely and critically observe the arrival of all those who visit these points—in terms of volume, manner of arrival, ease of navigation and the preferences, pleasure, frustration, embarrassment or awkwardness of those who enter. Fine tune the entrances accordingly. Then do it again. And again. Make it a habit.

Alternatively, if you seek to bait your audience by delivering yourself to them, for example setting up stall on a street corner, you may already realise the efficiency of fishing wisely. You prepare, locate and cast to suit, facing the possibility of talking to thin air.

Upmarket or downmarket, your self-management of space reveals how you value the space of others, for if space is a luxury for some, it represents wastage for others. There may also be no option: those with no choice but economy may be pressurised into utilising what little they have.

Defensive space

There is a need to defend an identity from mistreatment by its own organisation and others.

Start by determining the defendable space, which should surround your logo. This is the distance within which no other element may intrude. This method of spacing can then be applied when positioning another item, such as an address block, or other situations where space is limited.

Illustration 24

```
┌ ─ ─ ─ ─ ─ ─ ─ ─ ┐
│                 │
│     small       │
│                 │
└ ─ ─ ─ ─ ─ ─ ─ ─ ┘
```

```
┌ ─ ─ ─ ─ ─ ─ ─ ─ ─ ─ ─ ─ ─ ─ ─ ─ ─ ┐
│                                   │
│     E  X  P  A  N  S  I  V  E     │
│                                   │
└ ─ ─ ─ ─ ─ ─ ─ ─ ─ ─ ─ ─ ─ ─ ─ ─ ─ ┘
```

All logos should have a defensive area into which no other unauthorised graphic element—or edge of display area—may intrude.

Decide upon this convention of defendable space and whatever other rules are necessary to maintain the ideal amount of space to match the values of your identity.

Type

Voice

Typefaces imply character through their employment, management and control of space. Each typeface is a voice of character, often projecting itself beyond the content of the words being typeset. The best typography has grace and a certain invisibility: in other words it does not upstage the message being presented, but rather is a successful conduit through which the message is imparted, and with as little unsuitably false or negative bias as possible.

Some typefaces more than others exert a strong identity in their own right. A few become permanently associated with particular organisations or products. Indeed, many organisations operate with their own unique typeface—a font and font family cut especially for their usage. Owning the copyright has many advantages: they hopefully have a typeface designed to exactly fit their personal requirements, and one which, through use, may be uniquely associated with their identity, and no one else's. In addition, their ownership means they can distribute the typeface without paying licensing fees.

The distinction between one typeface and another may be due to subtleties of design too slight for most to notice or consciously care about. But the visual effect of one in relation to another becomes more obvious when comparing them side by side. A fast and effective way to judge the influence of a typeface to be used in text, therefore, is to compare it with blocks of other faces, as illustrated overleaf. The overall effect is to reveal more of its visual traits.

Illustration 25

Letterforms are the most important and essential means of conveying verbal information. They also carry emotional and aesthetic information which impacts on how the verbal message is read.

Letterforms are the most important and essential means of conveying verbal information. They also carry emotional and aesthetic information which impacts on how the verbal message is read.

Letterforms are the most important and essential means of conveying verbal information. They also carry emotional and aesthetic information which impacts on how the verbal message is read.

Letterforms are the most important and essential means of conveying verbal information. They also carry emotional and aesthetic information which...

Letterforms are the most important and essential means of conveying verbal information. They also carry emotional and...

Letterforms are the most important and essential means of conveying verbal information. They also carry emotional and aesthetic information which impacts on how the verbal message is read.

Each typeface creates and conveys different emotional and aesthetic information.

Pitch

Forgetting technical terms of differentiation, which determine one typestyle from another, typefaces can be swept into several broad categories. These can include fat, thin, squeezed, expanded, ornate, austere, clinical, humorous, serious, dull, bulky, readable and unreadable (dependent upon proportions and weight), as well as any other attitude, mood or pretence one wishes to name. Some shout, some whisper. Some are upmarket, others downmarket. Some have vintage, allude to a period of history or other association. Some are friendly, others foreboding. Select and experiment on the basis of decoration, weight and, finally, the shape of any key letters or characters within the names of the identity you are constructing.

Illustration 26

hello! hello
hello
hello
hello
hello

Every typeface is a voice of personality.

A group of typefaces within the same style can be referred to as a type family. A collection or combination from different families is a combination. Family or combination, if this group is to speak as a team, in unison, by contrast or complement, you must select the fonts with care. Also, space the typefaces with equal attention to detail, for the set (the space between characters) or leading (the space between each line) can radically alter the appearance of the same font.

The process of selecting the correct fonts for your identity is one of examining the intangibles contained by your firmwords. Certainly the majority of typefaces will be unsuitable for your identity. Insist on finding the perfect combination of typefaces for the task in hand.

Launch

Departure

A new identity is a departure. It is a break with what can now more clearly be seen as the tradition of yesterday—a noticeable change of direction, marginal or revolutionary, but a landmark in the culture of the organisation.

Departure points involve risk, though often against a background of no alternative other than persisting with the unworkable or inappropriate. Introducing the new requires preparation and concentration. The intention is to impose a new order. And just like any newly conquering force, the need is to plan well, for it is not just the launch but the domination and rule of law and order thereafter which should be of concern.

However notably this new order breaks with the past, it is unlikely to be a complete divorce from it, for traces of history tend to remain. This is not just in the short term, whilst the new identity establishes an invasion beachhead, but in the longer-term memories and attitudes of those who must live through the changes the identity will bring about.

Change, as ever, may threaten some of the audience and therefore requires the most careful explanation. You may easily be taken off-guard by their concerns. Some customers and suppliers may be subject to legal agreements which will need to be acknowledged, should you be changing your name, or if the changes in visual appearance may be construed as leading to confusion. Again, beware, for the new identity may confuse more than expected.

Audiences need to be led from one stability, or feeling of comfort, to another. You are about to lead them in the direction of your choosing. Some will complain during this journey, but this doesn't mean they will not follow. The art is to allow only those casualties you intend. The strains you are now placing upon them through the upheavals of change are authorised by you. A new identity is a new focus, and as such must also refocus your audience. Believers and disbelievers, disgruntled or newly motivated—a new identity will immediately alter the mentality of both your organisation and your audience.

At what speed you dispense with the past and usher in the new will depend on many factors. For many, with product in the field, the new identity will have no alternative but to operate alongside the old. This is not the problem it may seem to some, for if the old identity has any value at all, there will no doubt be some sympathy shown towards it within the new design. Regardless, the contrast between old and new may still be dramatic.

For small and medium-sized organisations, the phasing in of the new identity may be undertaken quickly and with the minimum of fuss. Alternatively, and more commonly, you may need to be expedient in the running down of old supplies. If so, orchestrate in as few a number of stages as possible. There will be wastage but, hopefully, the effect of the new identity will more than compensate.

For a very large organisation the identity will by necessity need to be introduced step-by-step because a project so important and long-lasting should not be hurried, and it is also normally not only unavoidable, but more cost-effective to do it this way. Depending upon the extent and complexity of the organisation's operations, a series of programmes may need to be launched—some, but not all, simultaneously—from the basic principles for stationery, sales promotion, literature, packaging and product identification to architectural, vehicle or transport identification, and so on. There may also be a need for publications or events to inform the rest of the organisation about the nature and progress of implementation.

Thought—last is often first.

Most pressure is self-inflicted. You create it and perhaps expect it, even demand it. There is always a reason for travelling faster. After all, you can see the benefits of the new identity before others. In your mind it exists already. The temptation not to hold back until the launch can be fully stage-managed is, for some, immense. The very process of creating identity creates pressure. Implementing and then launching tends to add to this sense of urgency. A launch date must be set which allows you to accommodate the necessary preparation and planning.

In the meantime, sundry renewal or stationery reprint requirements will inconveniently make demands upon you. It is wise not to let the interruption of such minor requirements upset the sequence of your planned launch. Keep a cool head. If necessary, prior to the official launch date, make whatever reprints necessary. Or, confront the fear of not responding—instead, make do without—it may be better! Keep the larger picture in mind rather than the pettiness of minor economics. The long-term worth of your identity is likely to be far more valuable than any temporary shortfall of brochures or stock of wasted letter headings.

A launch is an announcement. Public or private, full dress or casual, the function awaits you. A definite launch event is useful because it collects and concentrates the mind, bringing the culmination of your work to an inescapable deadline. The identity, its hope and fears, and those responsible for them, will be judged anew from the moment of the announcement. Speaking to a wide public or external audience is now a different matter compared to dwelling upon the same issues within the theoretically private walls of the steering group or wider organisation. The external pressures may be more destructive than the internal pressures experienced so far, but they complete the cylndrical process of criticism. By taking an identity to market you are declaring your readiness and quality of workmanship and management. If it is wrong now, you will potentially pay an extreme price.

The announcement of a new organisation differs from the re-identification of an existing organisation. There are also takeovers, where a new identity needs to be an adaptation, blend or complete submission to another existing identity. There are other issues to address when changing name, occupation or industry. There are product launches within the domain of an already successful corporate identity or related family of brands. The full extent of these permutations and the problems they pose seem endless.

The correct protocol or convenient pecking order for the identity's communication is a matter of manners and politics. Whatever the apparent complications, good manners suggest that it is wise to think internally first, externally second. Politics decides whether and in which order you include investors, staff, customers, prospective customers, suppliers, agencies, press and media.

Thought—there is no substitute for thoroughness except chaos.

Launching to these different audiences gives you three basic choices of attitude: talking down, up, or to equals. Whatever your decision, take care not to offend or upset the feelings of anyone more than necessary. Schedule in detail, co-ordinating the various elements and programme of events with patience and thoroughness.

Guidance

A sense of order is a basic requirement of any identity. To achieve this through design there needs to be an acknowledgement and adherence to a number of rules. A clear explanation of these laws to others is necessary if they are to both understand and then successfully follow. Without clearly stated laws and guidelines an identity cannot be effectively managed.

Thought—you create an identity to benefit the organisation in its entirety. You construct the laws and necessary guidelines to make this possible.

Most of those who need to communicate, propagate or be involved in the interpretation of the identity will need to be closely regulated. Many cannot be trusted to behave themselves otherwise. This is understandable. It is most commonly a cause of the inability to know any better, but there may also be factions whose attitude will be hostile, insurgent or obstinate because they wish to empire-build themselves, are jealous or insecure by nature, or else wish to escape what they see as the imposition of a foreign authority. Likewise, these elements may also seek to undermine any inadequacies in the content or presentation of the laws or guidelines themselves. They may believe that if they can disprove or render foolish even the smallest of written guidelines, they may succeed in undermining or fostering a wider-ranging condemnation of the authority controlling it. Of course, any failings brought to the attention of the authors should be received graciously, and constructive reportage and fault-finding is to be highly valued, indeed sought after. The issue is one of leadership: the recognition of loyalties and motives, and not over-reacting or responding inappropriately.

Thought—if you tire, you lose.

Even though you may state things clearly, there will still be those occasions when a reader will fail to understand—most probably because they hurried their reading. They may claim that you miss the point, when the point is there for all to see. They may claim that one instruction contradicts another, when, with a little more under-standing of the overall intent, they would realise that in fact it does not. They may disagree upon an item, word or instruction because of their entrapment by another persuasion—method or conven-tion—which you strenuously and intentionally disregard and chal-lenge. Their previous experience or training, though it may have some worthy values, may seek to oppose this new way forward, because it cannot take such a leap of faith as to knock away the foundations of their personal habit or tradition. To return to an earlier chapter, you have identified your position and prepared yourself for attack. The assaults do not disappear after a launch; an identity and its preservation are under a continual war of attrition.

Meanwhile, and on a more positive note, the more creative members of your team may be expected or invited to make their valued contribution towards the continuing development of the identity. Therefore the guidelines will need to allow a certain freedom, framework and procedure for these contributors to be able to exercise themselves.

In general, too much legislation can be tiresome and unnecessary. It can also be costly, for it involves added time for those whose job is to implement these laws. Yet having too few guidelines can lead to abuse of the intended identity through lack of sufficient instruction. This increases the chances of the identity suffering at the hands of others who, caring less than you, simply decide to interpret what rules there are to suit their own convenience. But the opposite of too much complexity can prove counter-productive if it demotivates those that are required to understand and fully implement. The ideal should be a virtuous circle, where the identity (your identity, their identity) inspires. In this regard, whatever the format of the guidelines—traditionally printed or electronically reproduced—the inspirational nature of the content and its ease of use greatly assist its effectiveness.

Where the detail of these guidelines ends, and the ability of management, staff and suppliers takes over, should be a matter of continued debate. This is because, by remaining interested in the aims of the project, you will make certain that the organisation continues to argue, build and maintain an identity which may radiate with clarity, distinction and purpose.

Distil the points you need to make until you can reduce no more. Even so, the volume of work in covering the necessary areas of instruction is usually fairly extensive. An identity is much more than the simple implementation of a logo. Many will have need to consult the guidelines: from those whose only wish is to create an overhead slide or word-processed document to those responsible for vehicle livery, signage, exhibitions or publicity brochures—all will benefit and thrive from clear instruction, or else have no choice but to produce their own interpretation of the law.

There will be eventualities that cannot be covered by any guidelines, however well planned in advance they may be. You need a communication channel available for clarification, further advice or the supply of additional materials. This can be someone internal to the organisation or external, providing, if externally based, they also belong to the original steering committee. This is necessary because continuity and authority is a requirement. The endorsement for this role should be given—and seen to be given—from the very top of the organisation. They should be a representative or ambassador of the organisation's leadership—nothing less. This indicates commitment and the understood ability to enforce the rules as necessary. It signals to all involved that their work or contribution to the working of the identity is both valued and judged by those in the highest authority. Failure to implement this process leads to neglect and carelessness, with the resultant lack of focus. The identity will wander and most likely be abused, unintentionally or otherwise, by those who will soon realise they are operating without enough instruction or feel free from any clear regulation. If the rules can be confused, ignored or overwritten at will, then there is no longer any form of planning permission. Your structure will be in danger because the engineering and maintenance of your identity is subject to a very different form of order—anarchy.

As the process of implementation takes place, issues of loyalty to the new ideal will be important to you. Loyalty for most people is determined by an identity's success. For those who must work with the new guidelines, their effect will soon become apparent. Despite any initial resistance, a noticeable increase in morale should follow. The definition for this success begins only as a measurement of opinion and faith, but this should soon give way to more tangible measurements—such as increased demand and profitability. In other words, a carefully prepared identity will work wonders for an organisation, if you are willing and patient enough to measure its effect.

For retailers, success or failure of an identity triggers a profit or loss more rapidly than any other areas of business operation. A failing shop with a poor identity, refitted yet selling the same stock, can potentially turn profit to loss with surprising alacrity. In other areas of business activity, the effects of identity and brand can take much longer to become apparent, which is the reason why you must closely manage its implementation.

Revisiting

Thought—new is never-ending.

An organisation needs to be kept informed about the issues that affect its identity. Information should be updated and distributed to those who need to be kept informed.

A launch date provides an anniversary—and often we may wonder whether we need the reminder of any anniversary, including this one—but such checkpoints are an important time for reflection, celebration or more sober reminder, all of which should help you preserve and maintain a safe and worthy destiny.

Consider that the identity launch was a success. Business is booming and you are on your way towards your cherished objectives. You have a firm grip upon the management and ongoing interpretation of the identity. You are able to judge for suitability each design and proposition that you encounter on your road ahead. You understand the visual ingredients, which together constitute your identity at its best. You understand the justification for your use of colour and shape. You are consistent, unbending in your desire, application and authority. The benefits of your identity are compounding daily. The original design appears to improve, demonstrating increasingly its

intelligent use when applied to the many facets of your organisation's communication requirements. You have entered into and
taken the identity to new levels of detail and glory. You are attentive
to the correct and incorrect, and continue to challenge all that you
do. The leading edge of your identity is the daily renewal which
confirms your design corresponds to the values and original inten-
tions. The course you originally set is maintained.

Great news, but things change in unforeseen ways.

An identity is linked to your product and services, marketing and
distribution. People change, events mould us. Technology invents
new methods of process and production, demand and abandonment. And so an identity must reassess itself in the light of the current experience, moulded by these continuing changes which are
thrust upon us. The newly important or commonly irritating problems which affect the identity, and which the current guidelines do
not adequately cover, should be acknowledged. If things are wrong
and the answers elude you, there should be a process of evaluation
and rectification. Guidelines must be updated to adapt, or else be
rendered obsolete. The management of the identity is in your
hands. You made the initial investment—it has been paying you
back in return. But that investment cannot and should not be just a
one-off. Your identity flourishes or dies according to the ongoing
attention you provide it with. It is your partner and friend. Take
good care of it if you want it to remain effective and loyal.

Finally

You have a choice: to compete or win. The two are different. The
former is compliance with a game where team spirit rules. You allow
and welcome competition because it is profitable to do so, or
because you fail to or choose not to consider the alternative: win-
ning. This is where there is only one focus: your killer instinct and
organisation's victory. Whichever option you choose, the truth is that
you are on your own. You are free to determine your own direction,
comply with your own guidelines or the guidelines of others, to

whatever tolerance of discipline or carelessness. The art of identity is to create that which is, or over time becomes, undeniably you. This living identity begins and ends with you. There is no delegation of responsibility for its understanding and maintenance. You source yourself to propel yourself.

That self, should you find it, is certain to be unique and powerful. Then you turn to the audience you wish to serve. With good fortune on your side, this audience cannot avoid you, nor would they wish to.

Why should they?

Index

i